The Wild Side
Close Calls

The Wild Side
Close Calls

Henry Billings

Melissa Billings

JAMESTOWN  PUBLISHERS

a division of NTC/CONTEMPORARY PUBLISHING GROUP

Lincolnwood, Illinois USA

ISBN 0–8092-9828-7

Published by Jamestown Publishers,
a division of NTC/Contemporary Publishing Group, Inc.
4255 West Touhy Avenue
Lincolnwood (Chicago), Illinois 60712-1975, U.S.A.

00 01 02 03 04 VL 10 9 8 7 6 5 4 3 2 1

CONTENTS

UNIT THREE

To the Student

We probably all know someone who has had a close call. Maybe a car crashed into the car right in front of that person. Or the airplane that he or she was supposed to be on exploded. That person was lucky, though. It was only a close call.

The articles in this book are about close calls. Some tell the stories of people who were caught in bomb explosions. Others are about people who were attacked by wild animals or lost in the wilderness. All of the people you will read about survived the experience, but it was a close call. They almost didn't make it. You will probably learn something from every article. You will come away from some of them with unanswered questions. You may be surprised or horrified. You may be skeptical or amazed. But you will not be bored.

As you read and enjoy the 15 articles in this book, you will be developing your reading skills. If you complete all the lessons in this book, you will surely increase your reading speed and improve your reading comprehension and critical thinking skills. Also, because these exercises include items of the types often found on state and national tests, learning how to complete them will prepare you for tests you may have to take in the future.

How to Use This Book

About the Book.   *Close Calls* contains three units, each of which includes five lessons. Each lesson begins with an article about an unusual subject or event. The article is followed by a group of four reading comprehension exercises and three critical thinking exercises. The reading comprehension exercises will help you understand the article. The critical thinking exercises will help you think about what you have read and how it relates to your own experience.

At the end of each lesson, you will also have the opportunity to give your personal response to some aspect of the article and then to assess how well you understood what you read.

The Sample Lesson.   Working through the sample lesson, the first lesson in the book, with your class or group will demonstrate how a lesson is organized. The sample lesson explains how to complete the exercises and score your answers. The correct answers for the sample exercises and sample scores are printed in lighter type. In some cases, explanations of the correct answers are given. The explanations will help you understand how to think through these question types.

If you have any questions about how to complete the exercises or score them, this is the time to get the answers.

Working Through Each Lesson.   Begin each lesson by looking at the photograph and reading the caption. Before you read, predict what you think the article will be about. Then read the article.

Sometimes your teacher may decide to time your reading. Timing helps you keep track of and increase your reading speed. If you have been timed, enter your reading time in the box at the end of the lesson. Then use the Words-per-Minute Table to find your reading speed and record your speed on the Reading Speed Graph at the end of the unit.

Next complete the Reading Comprehension and Critical Thinking exercises. The directions for each exercise will tell you how to mark your answers. When you have finished all four Reading Comprehension exercises, use the answer key provided by your teacher to check your work. Follow the directions after each exercise to find your score. Record your Reading Comprehension scores on the graph at the end of each unit. Then check your answers to the Author's Approach, Summarizing and Paraphrasing, and Critical Thinking exercises. Fill in the Critical Thinking Chart at the end of each unit with your evaluation of your work and comments about your progress.

At the end of each unit, you will also complete a Compare and Contrast Chart. The completed chart will help you see what the articles have in common, and it will give you an opportunity to explore your own ideas about the events in the articles.

SAMPLE
LESSON

Up, Up, and Away

Ever since he was a kid, Larry Walters had wanted to fly. But things didn't work out for him. His poor eyesight disqualified him from being a pilot. Instead, Walters became a truck driver. Still, he never gave up his dream of flying. At last, at the age of 33, he decided he could wait no longer. He was going to do something no one had ever done before. He would fly through the skies sitting in his lawn chair!

2   Lawn chairs, of course, are not meant to fly. That didn't bother Larry Walters. He had a plan to make one fly. He gathered 45 weather balloons and attached them to his chair. He intended

Larry Walters finally realizes his dream of flying—by tying helium balloons to a lawn chair.

to fill them with helium, a gas lighter than air. The balloons would then lift him—and his chair—up, up and away. Walters hoped to make it a few hundred feet into the air. He figured that he would float with the wind for a while before coming back to earth.

3   Walters set his launch date for July 2, 1982. His launch site was a backyard in San Pedro, California. At first, everything went as planned. Walters tied the balloons to the chair. Then friends held the chair down with ropes while he filled the balloons with helium.

4   Walters had no training in ballooning. Still, he knew enough to be prepared. He took a parachute with him. He also brought along a CB radio, some water, and a camera. Finally, Walters brought a BB gun. He figured that way he could pop some of the balloons when he was ready to land.

5   When Walters gave the signal, his friends dropped the ropes. The chair lifted off, with Walters sitting in it. But the balloons worked all too well. The chair shot straight up. The jolt knocked Walters's glasses off. "It kind of startled me when it let go," he later said.

6   Walters had hoped to get a few hundred feet off the ground. Soon, however, he was at 16,000 feet! He was flying high enough to be spotted by airline pilots. At that height, the air was freezing. Walters was wearing only a light jacket. Before he knew it, he was growing numb from the cold. He was also getting scared. The fun was over. Now all he thought about was how to get down safely.

7   Walters sent out a Mayday message over his CB radio. Then he used his BB gun to pop a few of the balloons. To his great relief, the chair started to come down. But there was still his landing to worry about.

8   Luckily, Walters did land in one piece. His lawn chair hit some power lines on the way down. That knocked out electricity in the area for 20 minutes. Yet somehow Walters walked away without a scratch. Except for a case of sunburn, he was unhurt. Later, Walters was asked why he did it. "It was something I had to do," he said. "I had this dream for 20 years. If I hadn't done it, I would have ended up in a funny farm."

9 Some people wondered if he planned to do it again. "I'm staying right on the ground," he answered when asked. "It was a one-shot deal. You couldn't pay me a million dollars to do it again."

10 Many people laughed at Walters's stunt. TV shows had him on to talk about his flight. A few people even called him a hero. Others were not so amused. Officials in charge of air safety were downright angry. The flying chair could have disrupted planes taking off and landing. That could have caused a tragic accident. Still, these officials didn't know quite what to do with Walters. "If he had a pilot's license, we'd suspend that," said one. "But he doesn't." Even so, they were sure he had broken some part of the law. "And as soon as we decide which part it is, some type of charge will be filed."

11 In the end, Walters paid a $1,500 fine. Air-safety officials said he had flown an unlicensed "aircraft." Also, they said he had flown too close to an airport. Larry Walters did, however, win recognition for his stunt. His flight earned him top prize from the Bonehead Club of Dallas.

If you have been timed while reading this article, enter your reading time below. Then turn to the Words-per-Minute Table on page 55 and look up your reading speed (words per minute). Enter your reading speed on the graph on page 56.

Reading Time: Sample Lesson

_____ : _____
Minutes   Seconds

A   Finding the Main Idea

One statement below expresses the main idea of the article. One statement is too general, or too broad. The other statement explains only part of the article; it is too narrow. Label the statements using the following key:

M—Main Idea   **B—Too Broad**   **N—Too Narrow**

___B___ 1. Larry Walters always wanted to fly. [This statement is true, but it is *too broad*. The story focuses on Walters's flight in a lawn chair.]

___N___ 2. Larry Walters flew to 16,000 feet in a lawn chair, angering air-safety officials. [This statement is true, but it is *too narrow*. It only gives a few of the details from the story.]

___M___ 3. Larry Walters received a lot of attention from airline officials and the media when he realized his lifelong dream to fly by tying helium balloons to a lawn chair. [This statement is the *main idea*. It tells you what the selection is about.]

___15___ Score 15 points for a correct M answer.

___10___ Score 5 points for each correct B or N answer.

___25___ **Total Score:** Finding the Main Idea

B   Recalling Facts

How well do you remember the facts in the article? Put an X in the box next to the answer that correctly completes each statement about the article.

1. Larry Walters didn't become a pilot because
   □ a. he was afraid of heights.
   ☒ b. his eyesight was not good enough.
   □ c. he was not smart enough.

2. The balloons tied to his chair carried Walters
   ☒ a. much higher than he expected.
   □ b. into the flight path of an airplane.
   □ c. above the clouds.

3. On his flight, Walters didn't use
   □ a. his BB gun.
   ☒ b. his parachute.
   □ c. his CB radio.

4. When people heard about Walters's flight,
   □ a. they were angry.
   □ b. they were amused.
   ☒ c. reactions were mixed.

5. Air-safety officials
   ☒ a. fined Walters for his stunt.
   □ b. suspended Walters's pilot's license.
   □ c. flew an unlicensed aircraft.

Score 5 points for each correct answer.

___25___ **Total Score:** Recalling Facts

C | Making Inferences

When you combine your own experience with information from a text to draw a conclusion that is not directly stated in that text, you are making an inference. Below are five statements that may or may not be inferences based on information in the article. Label the statements using the following key:

C—Correct Inference   F—Faulty Inference

_____C_____ 1. There are stricter eyesight requirements for pilots than for truck drivers. [This is a *correct* inference. You are told that Walters's eyesight was not good enough to be a pilot. He is a truck driver, so you can infer that the requirements are not as strict.]

_____C_____ 2. Larry Walters didn't know how much helium it would take to lift a lawn chair into the air. [This is a *correct* inference. You are told that Walters hoped to make it a few hundred feet in the air, yet he ended up 16,000 feet in the air.]

_____F_____ 3. Walters's parachute didn't work. [This is a *faulty* inference. The article does not say whether Walters tried to use his parachute.]

_____F_____ 4. Walters did his stunt so that he could get on TV. [This is a *faulty* inference. Although Walters did get on TV, the article states that he did his stunt because he had always wanted to fly.]

_____F_____ 5. Walters had never flown in a plane. [This is a *faulty* inference. You can infer that Walters never *piloted* a plane, but the article does not state whether he ever rode in a plane.]

Score 5 points for each correct answer.

___25___ **Total Score:** Making Inferences

D | Using Words Precisely

Each numbered sentence below contains an underlined word or phrase from the article. Following the sentence are three definitions. One definition is closest to the meaning of the underlined word. One definition is opposite or nearly opposite. Label those two definitions using the following key; do not label the remaining definition.

C—Closest   O—Opposite or Nearly Opposite

1. His poor eyesight <u>disqualified</u> him from being a pilot.
   ___O___ a. allowed
   _____ b. discouraged
   ___C___ c. prevented

2. Before he knew it, he was growing <u>numb</u> from the cold.
   ___C___ a. without feeling
   ___O___ b. sensitive
   _____ c. tired

3. That could have caused a <u>tragic</u> accident.
   _____ a. big
   ___C___ b. terrible
   ___O___ c. minor

4. "If he had a pilot's license, we'd <u>suspend</u> that."
   _____ a. take
   ___O___ b. let him keep
   ___C___ c. discontinue

5. "It kind of <u>startled</u> me when it let go."

_____ a. hurt

___O___ b. surprised

___C___ c. calmed

___15___	Score 3 points for each correct C answer.
___10___	Score 2 points for each correct O answer.
___25___	**Total Score:** Using Words Precisely

Enter the four total scores in the spaces below, and add them together to find your Reading Comprehension Score. Then record your Reading Comprehension Score on the graph on page 57.

Score	Question Type	Sample Lesson
___25___	Finding the Main Idea	
___25___	Recalling Facts	
___25___	Making Inferences	
___25___	Using Words Precisely	
___100___	**Reading Comprehension Score**	

Author's Approach

Put an X in the box next to the correct answer.

1. The main purpose of the first paragraph is to

☐ a. introduce Larry Walters.

☐ b. give the authors' opinion of Larry Walters.

☒ c. explain the motivation for Larry Walters's flight.

2. What do the authors imply by saying, "Yet somehow Walters walked away without a scratch"?

☐ a. It is surprising that Larry Walters was not scratched by trees as he came down.

☒ b. It is surprising that Larry Walters was not hurt as he came down.

☐ c. It is surprising that Walters could walk after he landed.

3. What is the authors' purpose in writing "Up, Up, and Away"?

☒ a. to entertain the reader

☐ b. to express an opinion about Larry Walters

☐ c. to persuade the reader not to fly in a lawn chair

___3___	Number of correct answers

Record your personal assessment of your work on the Critical Thinking Chart on page 58.

Summarizing and Paraphrasing

Follow the directions provided for questions 1 and 2. Put an X in the box next to the correct answer for question 3.

1. Complete the following one-sentence summary of the article using the lettered phrases from the phrase bank below.

Phrase bank:

a. a description of what happened after the flight

b. what happened when the lawn chair was launched

c. an explanation of how he prepared for his flight

The article about Larry Walters begins with _____c_____, goes on to explain _____b_____, and ends with _____a_____.

2. Reread paragraph 6 in the article. Below, write a summary of the paragraph in no more than 25 words.

[Explain the main ideas in paragraph 6.]

_____

_____

_____

_____

Reread your summary and decide whether it covers the important ideas in the paragraph. Next, decide how to shorten the summary to 15 words or less without leaving out any essential information. Write this summary below.

[Explain the main ideas in fewer words.]

_____

_____

_____

_____

3. Read the statement from the article below. Then read the paraphrase of that statement. Choose the reason that best tells why the paraphrase does not say the same thing as the statement.

Statement: "The flying chair could have disrupted planes taking off and landing."

Paraphrase: The flying chair got in the way of planes trying to take off and land.

☐ a. Paraphrase says too much.

☐ b. Paraphrase doesn't say enough.

☒ c. Paraphrase doesn't agree with the statement from the article. [The paraphrase states that the chair *did* get in the way of planes taking off and landing, but the statement only states that that was a possibility.]

____3____ Number of correct answers

Record your personal assessment of your work on the Critical Thinking Chart on page 58.

Critical Thinking

Put an X in the box next to the correct answer.

1. Which of the following statements from the article is an opinion rather than a fact?

☐ a. "The jolt knocked off Walters's glasses."

☒ b. "They were sure he had broken some part of the law."

☐ c. "His flight earned him top prize from the Bonehead Club of Dallas."

2. From the article, you can predict that

☐ a. many people wanted to fly in lawn chairs after seeing Walters's stunt.

☒ b. Larry Walters did not fly in a lawn chair again.

☐ c. Larry Walters never flew again.

3. What did you have to do to answer question 2?

☐ a. draw a conclusion (a sensible statement based on the text and your experience)

☐ b. find a purpose (why something is done)

☒ c. make a prediction (a decision on what is likely to happen based on information in the article)

4. What was the effect of popping a few of the balloons with a BB gun?

☐ a. The electricity was knocked out in the area for 20 minutes.

☒ b. The chair started to come down.

☐ c. Walters landed in one piece.

5. Of the following theme categories, which would this story fit into?

☐ a. flying machines

☒ b. fact is stranger than fiction

☐ c. courageous acts

____5____ Number of correct answers

Record your personal assessment of your work on the Critical Thinking Chart on page 58.

Personal Response

I can't believe . . .

[Write something you found hard to believe while reading the article.]

Self-Assessment

A word or phrase in the article that I do not understand is

[Write a word or phrase in the article that you did not understand.]

Self-Assessment

To get the most out of the *Wild Side* series program, you need to take charge of your own progress in improving your reading comprehension and critical thinking skills. Here are some of the features that help you work on those essential skills.

Reading Comprehension Exercises.   Complete these exercises immediately after reading each article. They help you recall what you have read, understand the stated and implied main ideas, and add words to your working vocabulary.

Critical Thinking Skills Exercises.   These exercises help you focus on the authors' approach and purpose, recognize and generate summaries and paraphrases, and identify relationships between ideas.

Personal Response and Self-Assessment.   Questions in this category help you relate the articles to your personal experience and give you the opportunity to evaluate your understanding of the information in that lesson.

Compare and Contrast Charts.   At the end of each unit you will complete a Compare and Contrast Chart. The completed chart helps you see what the articles have in common and gives you an opportunity to explore your own ideas about the topics discussed in the articles.

The Graphs.   The graphs and charts at the end of each unit enable you to keep track of your progress. Check your graphs regularly with your teacher. Decide whether your progress is satisfactory or whether you need additional work on some skills. What types of exercises are you having difficulty with? Talk with your teacher about ways to work on the skills in which you need the most practice.

UNIT ONE

Lost in the Maine Wilderness

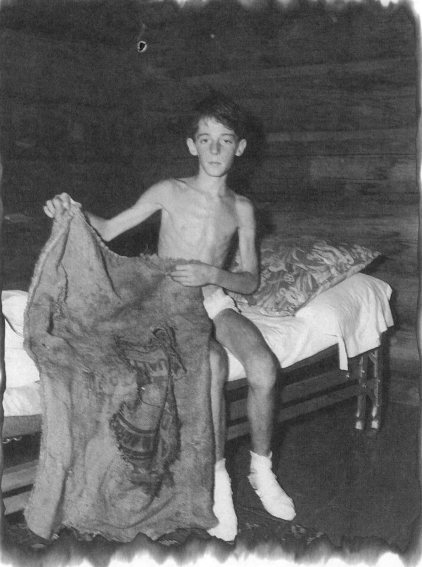

Donn Fendler knew exactly what he was doing. At least, he thought he did. The 12-year-old Fendler stood at the top of Maine's Mount Katahdin. He had rushed ahead of his father to get to the summit, but now fog was moving in. Fendler was nervous. He had heard of hikers getting lost on foggy mountaintops. So he began to hurry back down the trail, expecting to meet his father any minute. Without knowing it, however, Fendler took a wrong turn. He lost the trail. Instead of moving closer to his father, the boy was moving farther and farther away.

Hours after his rescue, Donn Fendler holds up the sack that he slept in during his days in the wilderness.

2 Soon Fendler found himself stumbling over big, jagged rocks. He didn't remember climbing over those rocks on his way up the mountain, and he realized he must have taken a wrong turn. The fog was so thick he couldn't see more than a few yards in any direction. He shouted as loud as he could, but there was no answer. He tried to run back the way he had come, but he wasn't sure which way that was. Panic began to set in. After all, he was a city boy. His home was in Rye, New York. All he knew about the wilderness was what little he had learned from his Boy Scout troop.

3 Crying now, Fendler slipped and fell. He scrambled to his feet and kept running. At last, when he was out of breath, he sat down on a rock and tried to think. As he later said, "The thing I had to do was figure out a plan and stick to it."

4 The plan he formed was a simple one. He would keep going until he found a trail or a stream. Then he would follow it down the mountain. Sooner or later, he figured, that would lead him to safety.

5 By this time, Fendler's father had realized his son was lost. Mr. Fendler and a few other hikers began to search for him, but they looked in all the wrong places. They thought Fendler would still be near the top of Mount Katahdin, on the south side. In fact, he was moving steadily down the north side of the 5,273-foot peak.

6 As the sun sank in the sky, the hikers knew they needed help. Mr. Fendler rushed to the base of the mountain. By morning a huge search was underway. For the next week hundreds of people combed the top of Mount Katahdin. They were all looking for a 74-pound boy wearing jeans and a light windbreaker. They found nothing.

7 The search failed because rescuers stuck to the top of Mount Katahdin. By the time the search began, Fendler was no longer near the top of the mountain. The very first day he got lost—July 17, 1939—he made it down below the tree line. That put him far from the search parties. In fact, within a couple of days Fendler left the mountain altogether and began wandering through the Maine wilderness.

8 That first night a storm blew in. Winds rose to 40 miles per hour. Sleet and hail fell. The temperature dropped to about 40 degrees. Fendler took off his wet pants and sneakers. Then he curled up under a big tree and cried himself to sleep.

9 He woke up at dawn, wet, cold, and hungry. He tried to put on his sneakers, but the soles were completely shredded. They had been cut to ribbons by the sharp rocks he had climbed over the day before. To make matters worse, his pants were still soaking wet. So Fendler picked up the wet pants and torn sneakers and set off, barefoot and bare-legged.

10 By the middle of the second day, the rain had stopped, but Fendler now faced a new problem. An endless swarm of mosquitoes and black flies swarmed around his head. Huge biting moose flies attacked him too. He tried to swat them away, but it was impossible. There were just too many of them. Within hours his body was swollen with bites. "My wrists were covered with blood from the mosquitoes I'd smashed," he later

said. "I had a million bites. I looked like I had measles or smallpox."

11 Later that day Fendler came to a berry patch. He fell to his hands and knees, shoving ripe berries into his mouth. It was the first time he'd found anything to eat since getting lost. By then his feet were badly swollen and his whole body ached. As night fell, Fendler crawled into a hollow tree and cried himself to sleep.

12 The next day Fendler found a stream. His hopes rose. Surely it would soon lead him to a cabin or a campground or a group of fishermen. Hour after hour he followed it. Sometimes he waded through the cold water. Other times he scrambled along the large rocks that dotted the bank. Once he fell and hurt his hip. But he got to his feet and continued on.

13 The next several days were much the same. Fendler hobbled along the edge of the stream, growing weaker by the hour. He ate berries whenever he found them. Other than that, he had nothing in his stomach but water from the stream. Somewhere along the way he dropped his sneakers and his pants. It didn't matter. They weren't any good to him anymore.

14 Each night he lay down under a tree. He always curled up tight, trying to stay warm. He covered himself with an old sack he had found. Each

morning he awoke to find himself covered with fresh bug bites. He scratched his legs until they were raw and bleeding. The scratches became infected and were soon throbbing with pain.

15 On the fifth day he spotted a cabin among the trees. He wanted to shout with happiness. He thought that at last his ordeal was over. He eagerly made his way over to the cabin. But when he arrived, he found that it was old and deserted. Obviously no one had been there for years. Discouraged, Fendler continued on down the stream.

16 Once he collapsed in an open space and slept for hours. When he woke up, he found that the backs of his legs were badly sunburned. Later, he fell into a deep section of the stream. When he managed to climb out, his body was covered with leeches.

17 By this time Fendler was quite weak. He hadn't eaten anything but berries for almost a week and had walked several miles each day. It was amazing he was even alive. Back up on Mount Katahdin, most of the searchers had given up hope. The few who kept looking were searching for a dead body.

18 Yet Fendler did not give up. Somehow he managed to stagger along. He lost all track of time. He saw bears and deer and other animals but paid them little attention. He was

getting dizzier and dizzier. He barely had the energy left to cry.

19 Then at last, on July 25, he saw another cabin in the distance. To his joy and relief, a man emerged from it. Fendler shouted. The man ran to his canoe, jumped in, and paddled over to Fendler as fast as he could.

20 And so Donn Fendler was rescued at last. He was found 35 miles from the base of Mount Katadin. In all, he had wandered over 90 miles through some of the country's most desolate landscape. His weight had dropped from 74 pounds to 58 pounds. The amazing story of how he survived was later told in a book called *Lost on a Mountain in Maine*.

If you have been timed while reading this article, enter your reading time below. Then turn to the Words-per-Minute Table on page 55 and look up your reading speed (words per minute). Enter your reading speed on the graph on page 56.

Reading Time: Lesson 1

——— : ———
Minutes   Seconds

A │ Finding the Main Idea

One statement below expresses the main idea of the article. One statement is too general, or too broad. The other statement explains only part of the article; it is too narrow. Label the statements using the following key:

M—Main Idea   B—Too Broad   N—Too Narrow

_____ 1. Donn Fendler took a wrong turn while hiking and found himself wandering for eight days in the Maine wilderness before being found.

_____ 2. It is amazing that Donn Fendler survived his ordeal in the Maine wilderness.

_____ 3. Donn Fendler ate only berries during the time he was lost in the Maine wilderness.

_____ Score 15 points for a correct M answer.

_____ Score 5 points for each correct B or N answer.

_____ **Total Score:** Finding the Main Idea

B │ Recalling Facts

How well do you remember the facts in the article? Put an X in the box next to the answer that correctly completes each statement about the article.

1. When Fendler realized he was lost,
   ☐ a. he began stumbling over big, jagged rocks.
   ☐ b. he sat down to figure out what to do.
   ☐ c. his father still had not reached the mountain top.

2. The people searching for Fendler
   ☐ a. were looking in the wrong places.
   ☐ b. didn't look high enough on the mountain.
   ☐ c. looked for him on the north side of the mountain.

3. The first night that Fendler was alone on the mountain,
   ☐ a. he shredded the soles of his shoes.
   ☐ b. the temperature dropped about 40 degrees.
   ☐ c. he cried himself to sleep.

4 One of the biggest problems Fendler encountered in the wilderness was
   ☐ a. bears.
   ☐ b. mosquitoes and flies.
   ☐ c. rain.

5. After Fendler fell into the stream he was following, he
   ☐ a. found leeches all over his body.
   ☐ b. decided not to follow it anymore.
   ☐ c. had difficulty climbing back out.

Score 5 points for each correct answer.

_____ **Total Score:** Recalling Facts

5

10

C Making Inferences

When you combine your own experience with information from a text to draw a conclusion that is not directly stated in that text, you are making an inference. Below are five statements that may or may not be inferences based on information in the article. Label the statements using the following key:

C—Correct Inference   F—Faulty Inference

_____ 1. Donn Fendler was not an experienced hiker.

_____ 2. None of the rescuers considered that Donn Fendler might have started down the mountain.

_____ 3. Berries were one of Fendler's favorite foods.

_____ 4. Fendler's father did not think he would see his son again.

_____ 5. Fendler had hiked in the Maine countryside before.

Score 5 points for each correct answer.

_____ **Total Score:** Making Inferences

D Using Words Precisely

Each numbered sentence below contains an underlined word or phrase from the article. Following the sentence are three definitions. One definition is closest to the meaning of the underlined word. One definition is opposite or nearly opposite. Label those two definitions using the following key; do not label the remaining definition.

C—Closest   O—Opposite or Nearly Opposite

1. He had rushed ahead of his father to the <u>summit</u>.

_____ a. top

_____ b. camp

_____ c. base

2. Soon Fendler found himself stumbling over big, <u>jagged</u> rocks.

_____ a. high

_____ b. smooth

_____ c. rough

3. <u>Panic</u> began to set in.

_____ a. calm

_____ b. hunger

_____ c. fear

4. Fendler <u>hobbled</u> along the edge of the stream, growing weaker by the hour.

_____ a. moved unsteadily

_____ b. strolled

_____ c. fell

5. In all, he had wandered over 90 miles through some of the country's most <u>desolate</u> landscape.

_____ a. lush

_____ b. dangerous

_____ c. gloomy

_____ Score 3 points for each correct C answer.

_____ Score 2 points for each correct O answer.

_____ **Total Score:** Using Words Precisely

Enter the four total scores in the spaces below, and add them together to find your Reading Comprehension Score. Then record your score on the graph on page 57.

Score	Question Type	Lesson 1
_____	Finding the Main Idea	
_____	Recalling Facts	
_____	Making Inferences	
_____	Using Words Precisely	
_____	**Reading Comprehension Score**	

Author's Approach

Put an X in the box next to the correct answer.

1. The authors probably wrote this article in order to

☐ a. explain why Donn Fendler shouldn't have left his father.

☐ b. show how amazing it was that Donn Fendler survived his ordeal.

☐ c. demonstrate how to survive in the wilderness.

2. The authors tell this story mainly by

☐ a. showing different points of view.

☐ b. using their imagination and creativity.

☐ c. retelling Donn Fendler's personal experiences.

3. The main purpose of the first paragraph is to

☐ a. explain how Donn Fendler got lost.

☐ b. introduce Donn Fendler.

☐ c. describe the dangers of hiking on Mount Katahdin.

_____ Number of correct answers

Record your personal assessment of your work on the Critical Thinking Chart on page 58.

CRITICAL THINKING

Summarizing and Paraphrasing

Follow the directions provided for question 1. Put an X in the box next to the correct answer for questions 2 and 3.

1. Look for the important ideas and events in paragraphs 8 and 9. Summarize those paragraphs in one or two sentences.

_____

_____

_____

_____

2. Below are summaries of the article. Choose the summary that says all the most important things about the article but in the fewest words.

☐ a. Donn Fendler got lost while hiking on Mount Katahdin and ended up walking over 90 miles and losing 16 pounds in eight days before he was found.

☐ b. Donn Fendler got lost when he was hiking down from the summit of Mount Katahdin. He suffered through eight days of rain, bug bites, sunburn, leeches, and loneliness before being found. By that time he had hiked about 90 miles and lost 16 pounds.

☐ c. Donn Fendler was lucky to have survived his days wandering the Maine wilderness.

3. Choose the sentence that correctly restates the following sentence from the article:

"The thing I had to do was figure out a plan and stick to it."

☐ a. I had to decide what to do.

☐ b. I had to keep going in the direction I was going.

☐ c. I had to decide what the best plan would be and follow it.

_____ Number of correct answers

Record your personal assessment of your work on the Critical Thinking Chart on page 58.

Critical Thinking

Put an X in the box next to the correct answer.

1. Which of the following statements from the article is an opinion rather than a fact?

☐ a. Soon Fendler found himself stumbling over big, jagged rocks.

☐ b. They thought Fendler would still be near the top of Mount Katahdin, on the south side.

☐ c. He ate berries whenever he found them.

2. What caused Donn Fendler to get lost?

☐ a. He was nervous.

☐ b. He took a wrong turn.

☐ c. He couldn't see his father.

3. What did you have to do to answer question 2?

☐ a. find an effect (something that happened)

☐ b. find a contrast (how things are different)

☐ c. find a cause (why something happened)

4. From the article, you can conclude that if Donn Fendler had stayed near the top of the mountain,

☐ a. the searchers would have found him.

☐ b. he would not have gotten lost.

☐ c. he would not have reached the summit.

5. Of the following theme categories, which would this story fit into?

☐ a. young boys' adventures

☐ b. how to survive in the wilderness

☐ c. mountain-climbing techniques

_____ Number of correct answers

Record your personal assessment of your work on the Critical Thinking Chart on page 58.

Personal Response

I know how Donn Fendler felt in this story because

_____

_____

_____

_____

Self-Assessment

From reading this article, I have learned

_____

_____

_____

_____

Shipwrecked Dreams

Peter and Doreen Cheek shared a dream. They wanted to sail around the world together. The Cheeks were in no hurry. They wanted to savor each moment. So the British couple planned to take five full years to complete their journey. But things didn't work out as they had planned. Halfway through their journey, the Cheeks' dream turned into a nightmare.

2   When they set out in 1995, Peter was 60 years old. Doreen was 56. For nearly $2\frac{1}{2}$ years, they sailed their boat, *Talis II*, from place to place. By 1998

Tasmania, an island south of Australia, has a rocky coastline and is surrounded by wild waters like those around Maatsuyker Island, where Peter and Doreen Cheek were shipwrecked.

they had made it to the other side of the world. They began exploring the sea south of Australia. The water there is often very rough, but the Cheeks knew what they were doing. They were both skilled sailors. They had been sailing most of their lives. As their daughter Sue said, "Their boat was like a member of the family."

3   The Cheeks also knew the dangers of the sea firsthand. Years earlier, during a boat race, Doreen had nearly drowned. A wave had washed her off the deck of *Talis II*. Other sailors had died in that race. Doreen only saved herself by grabbing a rope that was dangling off the end of the boat.

4   Now, on February 17, 1998, Doreen and Peter both found themselves at the mercy of the sea. They had sailed south of an Australian island called Maatsuyker. It was a rocky and remote place. But it was home to seals and sea lions, and Peter and Doreen wanted to film them. So they dropped anchor off shore. It was about 2:30 A.M. The night was pitch black.

5   All at once, the wind shifted. Despite the anchor, the sea began to push the boat toward some jagged

rocks. Seaweed clogged the propeller. That killed the engine. With no power, Peter and Doreen were helpless. They could not stop the boat from smashing into the rocks. All they could do was abandon ship before the crash came.

6   Quickly, the Cheeks got ready to leave the *Talis II*. They would have to set out in their small lifeboat, called a dinghy. First, Peter sent a brief radio message asking for help. Then, while Doreen put on her life jacket, Peter tossed his into the dinghy. They scooped up all their valuables and threw them into a bag. The bag, too, went into the dinghy. Then the Cheeks themselves hopped into the dinghy and headed for the shore of Maatsuyker. They never made it. The sea was much too rough. "The dinghy was just sucked down and driven under a crevice," Peter said later.

7   Within seconds, Peter and Doreen tumbled into the sea. Peter saw his life jacket bob up. He grabbed it. He and Doreen knew they had to get out of the water fast or they would drown. They couldn't make it all the way to Maatsuyker Island. The best they

could do was climb onto the pile of rocks that had just smashed their boat. Peter grabbed a handful of seaweed growing on the rocks. He pulled himself up out of the water. Doreen tried to follow, but she wasn't quite strong enough. So she grabbed onto her husband's leg. Using all his strength, Peter pulled her up.

8   The Cheeks then moved onto a larger rock. Since it was still night, all they could do was wait. They hoped that someone had heard their radio message. But Peter wasn't so sure. "I was worried that my Mayday call would be taken as a joke," he later said. "I hadn't really made clear that we were desperate. We were scared no one would turn up looking for us."

9   It was very cold on the rock, so Peter and Doreen covered themselves with clumps of grass to try to stay warm. Then they pondered the coming day. In a few hours, the sun would be up. But then what? If no help came, should they jump into the water and try to swim to the island? It wasn't far away, but the water was rough. They could easily be swept away. On the other hand, how long could they survive on this rock?

10   As it turned out, they did not have to make the daring swim to the island. Someone on another boat had heard Peter's message. Help was on the way. A plane was sent out from the Australian mainland. The pilot circled the area but failed to see the couple. Then, at dawn, Trevor Quint, a lighthouse keeper on the island, spotted the mast of the Cheeks' ruined boat sticking out of the water. Looking more closely, he saw Peter and Doreen clinging to the rocks. Peter also saw Quint.

11   "We're shipwrecked!" Peter yelled at Quint across the water.

12   "I can see that!" Quint yelled back.

13   Quint tried to reach the couple by boat. But he could barely get within 25 yards of them. The sea was too strong. Also, the seals posed a problem. They were nursing their pups. Quint knew they might attack anyone who came too close to their babies.

14   At last, after Peter and Doreen had spent nearly 10 hours on the rock, a rescue helicopter arrived. The crew lifted the Cheeks to safety. The pilot declared that the sea was the worst he had seen in his 23 years of rescue work. He said that Peter and Doreen were lucky to be alive. "No one goes down there [to this part of the ocean]," he said. "It's very, very wild."

15   Although the Cheeks were alive, their dream of sailing around the world was gone. Everything they owned was now at the bottom of the sea. "We've lost everything. All our photographs, clothes, gifts for our family—everything. It's all just gone forever," said Doreen. "The boat was not even insured."

16   Still, they were alive. That alone made them very lucky. As their daughter Sue said, "The gods seem to be on their side."

If you have been timed while reading this article, enter your reading time below. Then turn to the Words-per-Minute Table on page 55 and look up your reading speed (words per minute). Enter your reading speed on the graph on page 56.

Reading Time: Lesson 2

_____ : _____
Minutes   Seconds

A | Finding the Main Idea

One statement below expresses the main idea of the article. One statement is too general, or too broad. The other statement explains only part of the article; it is too narrow. Label the statements using the following key:

M—Main Idea   **B—Too Broad**   **N—Too Narrow**

_____ 1. Peter and Doreen Cheek's dream to sail around the world didn't work out.

_____ 2. The Cheeks' boat crashed in the rough waters off the Australian island of Maatsuyker.

_____ 3. Peter and Doreen Cheek's dream to sail around the world was interrupted when their boat smashed into rocks south of Australia.

_____ Score 15 points for a correct M answer.

_____ Score 5 points for each correct B or N answer.

_____ **Total Score:** Finding the Main Idea

B | Recalling Facts

How well do you remember the facts in the article? Put an X in the box next to the answer that correctly completes each statement about the article.

1. By the time they set out on their journey around the world,
☐ a. Peter Cheek had already nearly drowned once.
☐ b. the Cheeks knew they wouldn't make it.
☐ c. the Cheeks were already experienced sailors.

2. The Cheeks stopped off the shore of the island of Maatsuyker because
☐ a. the water was rough.
☐ b. it was getting dark.
☐ c. they wanted to film some seals and sea lions.

3. The Cheeks could not stop their boat from smashing into rocks because
☐ a. seaweed had clogged the engine's propeller.
☐ b. the wind had shifted.
☐ c. the sea had become too strong.

4. The Cheeks did not know if they would be rescued because
☐ a. they were in a remote location.
☐ b. Peter didn't think his Mayday call had sounded desperate enough.
☐ c. the waters around Maatsuyker were very rough.

5. The couple was finally rescued by a
☐ a. plane from the Australian mainland.
☐ b. lighthouse keeper from Maatsuyker Island.
☐ c. rescue helicopter.

Score 5 points for each correct answer.

_____ **Total Score:** Recalling Facts

C | Making Inferences

When you combine your own experience with information from a text to draw a conclusion that is not directly stated in that text, you are making an inference. Below are five statements that may or may not be inferences based on information in the article. Label the statements using the following key:

C—Correct Inference   F—Faulty Inference

_____ 1. The Cheeks were not easily frightened.

_____ 2. The Cheeks were not well prepared for their trip around the world.

_____ 3. This was not the first time the Cheeks had been in a boat accident.

_____ 4. Doreen Cheek did not know how to swim.

_____ 5. The Cheeks did not try to sail around the world a second time.

> Score 5 points for each correct answer.
>
> _____ **Total Score:** Making Inferences

D | Using Words Precisely

Each numbered sentence below contains an underlined word or phrase from the article. Following the sentence are three definitions. One definition is closest to the meaning of the underlined word. One definition is opposite or nearly opposite. Label those two definitions using the following key; do not label the remaining definition.

C—Closest   O—Opposite or Nearly Opposite

1. They wanted to <u>savor</u> each moment.

_____ a. rush

_____ b. enjoy

_____ c. taste

2. They were both <u>skilled</u> sailors.

_____ a. smart

_____ b. new

_____ c. experienced

3. Doreen only saved herself by grabbing a rope that was <u>dangling</u> off the end of the boat.

_____ a. hanging

_____ b. falling

_____ c. attached

4. It was a rocky and <u>remote</u> place.

_____ a. far away

_____ b. easy to reach

_____ c. harsh

5. All they could do was <u>abandon</u> the ship before the crash came.

_____ a. stop

_____ b. return to

_____ c. leave

_____ Score 3 points for each correct C answer.

_____ Score 2 points for each correct O answer.

_____ **Total Score:** Using Words Precisely

Enter the four total scores in the spaces below, and add them together to find your Reading Comprehension Score. Then record your score on the graph on page 57.

Score	Question Type	Lesson 2
_____	Finding the Main Idea	
_____	Recalling Facts	
_____	Making Inferences	
_____	Using Words Precisely	
_____	**Reading Comprehension Score**	

Author's Approach

Put an X in the box next to the correct answer.

1. The main purpose of the first paragraph is to .

☐ a. describe Peter and Doreen Cheek.

☐ b. give background information about the story.

☐ c. entertain the reader.

2. Which of the following statements from the article best describes the area around the island of Maatsuyker?

☐ a. The water there is often very rough.

☐ b. Doreen and Peter both found themselves at the mercy of the sea.

☐ c. "No one goes down there [to this part of the ocean]."

3. What is the authors' purpose in writing "Shipwrecked Dreams"?

☐ a. to express an opinion about the Cheeks' journey

☐ b. to describe the Cheeks' journey

☐ c. to entertain the reader

_____ Number of correct answers

Record your personal assessment of your work on the Critical Thinking Chart on page 58.

Summarizing and Paraphrasing

Follow the directions provided for question 1. Put an X in the box next to the correct answer for questions 2 and 3.

1. Reread paragraph 6 in the article. Below, write a summary of the paragraph in no more than 25 words.

_____

_____

_____

_____

Reread your summary and decide whether it covers the important ideas in the paragraph. Next, decide how to shorten the summary to 15 words or less without leaving out any essential information. Write this summary below.

_____

_____

_____

_____

2. Read the statement from the article below. Then read the paraphrase of that statement. Choose the reason that best tells why the paraphrase does not say the same thing as the statement.

   Statement: "The Cheeks also knew the dangers of the sea firsthand."

   Paraphrase: The Cheeks knew that the sea could be dangerous.

   ☐ a. Paraphrase says too much.

   ☐ b. Paraphrase doesn't say enough.

   ☐ c. Paraphrase doesn't agree with the statement from the article.

3. Choose the sentence that correctly restates the following sentence from the article: "'The dinghy was just sucked down and driven under a crevice,' Peter said later."

   ☐ a. The sea pulled the dinghy down under a rock.

   ☐ b. The dinghy sank until it got stuck under a rock.

   ☐ c. The Cheeks tried to drive the dinghy away from the rocks, but were pulled under the water.

_____ Number of correct answers

Record your personal assessment of your work on the Critical Thinking Chart on page 58.

Critical Thinking

Put an X in the box next to the correct answer for questions 1, 2, and 5. Follow the directions provided for questions 3 and 4.

1. Which of the following statements from the article is an opinion rather than a fact?

☐ a. They began exploring the sea south of Australia.

☐ b. The pilot circled the area but failed to see the couple.

☐ c. The pilot declared that the sea was the worst he had seen in his 23 years of rescue work.

2. From the information in the article, you can conclude that the Cheeks

☐ a. did not complete their trip around the world.

☐ b. did not sail again after their crash.

☐ c. recovered their boat, the *Talis II.*

3. Choose from the letters below to correctly complete the following statement. Write the letters on the lines.

   According to paragraph 10, _____ because _____.

   a. a lighthouse keeper took his boat out

   b. an Australian pilot did not rescue the Cheeks

   c. he didn't see them

4. Choose from the letters below to correctly complete the following statement. Write the letters on the lines.

   On the positive side, _____, but on the negative side, _____.

   a. they lost all their belongings

   b. the Cheeks were both skilled sailors

   c. the Cheeks survived the crash

5. What did you have to do to answer question 4?

☐ a. find a purpose (why something is done)

☐ b. find a cause (why something happened)

☐ c. find a contrast (how things are different)

_____ Number of correct answers

Record your personal assessment of your work on the Critical Thinking Chart on page 58.

Personal Response

I know the feeling

_____

_____

Self-Assessment

What concepts or ideas from the article were difficult?

_____

_____

Which were easy?

_____

_____

Hit by a Bullet

On July 2, 1994, life was looking pretty good for Kim Williams. She was playing the best golf of her life. Her drives were long and straight. Her chips and putts were right on the mark. For once, she felt as if she could beat anyone.

2   This was quite a change for Williams. Until this point she had not had much luck. In six years as a professional golfer, she had struggled. Her total winnings were just $23,077. Williams had not won a single tournament. In fact, she had never

Golfer Kim Williams signs autographs for her fans. Shortly after being shot in the neck by a hunter's stray bullet, Williams returned to the golf course to play one of the best games of her career.

come close. It was now halfway through the 1994 season. Again, she had started the year poorly. She had failed to finish among the top 20 golfers in her first 14 tournaments.

3   But at the Youngstown-Warren Classic she turned her game around. Things looked better—much better. The Classic is a three-day, 54-hole tournament. Williams had a great first day. On the second day it rained. The women had to stop playing after just 10 holes. But at last Williams was up with the leaders. She was just two strokes behind. She felt poised to win for the first time. Better yet, she was on the verge of cashing her first big paycheck.

4   That night, Williams headed to a drugstore. She needed some baby oil. She used the oil on her putter. The oil kept the club from getting rusty when it rained.

5   As Williams walked toward the store entrance, she suddenly felt a sharp pain in the left side of her neck. "It felt like somebody hit a baseball line drive into me," she later said.

6   "What was that?" she asked herself.

7   For a split second, she thought it might have been a golf ball. But she

wasn't on a golf course. She was standing on a sidewalk next to a parking lot. "Then I put my hand up to my neck and pulled it down," she said. "It was covered with blood." Only then did she realize what had happened. She had been shot!

8   Williams walked into the drugstore. She was still in a daze and not quite sure what to do. She asked someone to call 911. Then she slumped to the floor. A man grabbed some paper towels. Pressing them to Williams's neck, he tried to stop the bleeding.

9   "Oh my God, I'm going to bleed to death!" she remembered thinking.

10   A few minutes later, an ambulance arrived. Williams was rushed to the hospital. The police also hurried to the scene. They had lots of questions but few answers. Where had the shot come from? Who had fired it? Why would anyone want to shoot Williams?

11   At first, it seemed that Kim Williams might have been the victim of a drive-by shooting. In other words, someone might have driven by and shot at her from a car window. But the next day the police learned the truth.

The shooting had been a bizarre accident. A man from a nearby township confessed to the crime. He had been taking target practice in the woods about a mile away. One of his bullets missed the target. It flew out of the woods and struck Kim Williams in the neck.

12 When Williams arrived at the hospital, doctors quickly went to work on her. They discovered that the bullet was lodged against her esophagus. Yet they couldn't believe how lucky she was. The bullet hadn't hit any organs. The doctors took several tests. At last, they decided not to take the bullet out. It was too risky. The operation might do more harm than good. Instead, they decided to wait and see how she healed with the bullet still inside her.

13 For the next several hours, Williams drifted in and out of sleep. At first she was listed in only "fair" condition, but she grew more stable with each passing minute. At one point a nurse came in and looked at Williams's chart. It showed that Williams was getting better much faster than anyone expected. "Wow!" the nurse exclaimed. "You had an angel on your shoulder."

14 Williams agreed. Later she said she could feel the bullet every time she swallowed. But at least she was alive.

"I feel lucky," she said. "There's really no explanation for it. It's a miracle that a bullet can go through your neck and not hit anything."

15 After just two days in the hospital, Williams was released. She had a bright red scar on her neck. It hurt to move her head. Her legs felt weak. Still, she wanted to get right back out and start playing golf again. She had missed the end of the Youngstown-Warren Classic. But another tournament was coming up the following weekend. It was called the Jamie Farr Toledo Classic. To everyone's surprise, Williams entered it.

16 Williams wasn't sure she would have the strength to make it around the course. But somehow she did. In the first round, she shot an 18-hole score of 68. That tied her best score for the year. She was so tired at the end of the round that she nearly collapsed. She had to be driven to the first-aid tent for fluids and rest. She said her fatigue was "frightening." Her legs felt "like Jell-O." Nonetheless, she didn't drop out.

17 Williams went on to play the last two rounds. Again, she did very well. She shot a 72 followed by a 70. That was good enough to tie for 10th place. It was her best finish of the year. She won almost $10,000 in the tournament.

18 Williams found that the accident had made her famous. Several different news organizations wanted to report her story. People who had never heard of her before now called her by name. As one friend said, "At least everyone knows you're Kim Williams now."

19 Williams even found she could joke a bit about the shooting. "I don't mean to make fun," she later said, "but I might endorse Target Drug Stores." Or perhaps she could endorse Bullet golf clubs. She could give new meaning to their slogan, "No. 1 with a bullet."

A | Finding the Main Idea

One statement below expresses the main idea of the article. One statement is too general, or too broad. The other statement explains only part of the article; it is too narrow. Label the statements using the following key:

M—Main Idea   **B—Too Broad**   **N—Too Narrow**

_____ 1. Golfer Kim Williams was hit by a stray bullet while walking into a drugstore.

_____ 2. After surviving a freak shooting accident, professional golfer Kim Williams's game improved and she became famous.

_____ 3. The bullet that hit Kim Williams was shot by a man taking target practice in the woods about a mile away from where Williams was standing.

_____ Score 15 points for a correct M answer.

_____ Score 5 points for each correct B or N answer.

_____ **Total Score:** Finding the Main Idea

B | Recalling Facts

How well do you remember the facts in the article? Put an X in the box next to the answer that correctly completes each statement about the article.

1. At the Youngstown-Warren Classic in 1994, Kim Williams
   - ☐ a. was playing poorly.
   - ☐ b. won $10,000.
   - ☐ c. was playing the best golf of her life.

2. When Williams was shot, she
   - ☐ a. didn't realize what had happened at first.
   - ☐ b. went into a drugstore and called 911.
   - ☐ c. immediately slumped to the ground.

3. The bullet that hit Williams
   - ☐ a. lodged itself in her esophagus.
   - ☐ b. didn't hit any organs.
   - ☐ c. was removed in a risky operation.

4. In the Jamie Farr Toledo Classic, Williams
   - ☐ a. tied for 10th place.
   - ☐ b. collapsed on the golf course.
   - ☐ c. could not play the last two rounds of the tournament.

5. After the accident, Williams
   - ☐ a. began endorsing sports products.
   - ☐ b. stopped playing golf.
   - ☐ c. became famous.

_____ Score 5 points for each correct answer.

_____ **Total Score:** Recalling Facts

C Making Inferences

When you combine your own experience with information from a text to draw a conclusion that is not directly stated in that text, you are making an inference. Below are five statements that may or may not be inferences based on information in the article. Label the statements using the following key:

C—Correct Inference   F—Faulty Inference

_____ 1. Bullets can travel farther than a mile.

_____ 2. A person can't live with a bullet in his or her body.

_____ 3. The bullet helped Williams's golf game.

_____ 4. Williams became one of the best female golfers in the United States after being shot.

_____ 5. The man who shot Williams was sent to prison.

Score 5 points for each correct answer.

_____ **Total Score:** Making Inferences

D Using Words Precisely

Each numbered sentence below contains an underlined word or phrase from the article. Following the sentence are three definitions. One definition is closest to the meaning of the underlined word. One definition is opposite or nearly opposite. Label those two definitions using the following key; do not label the remaining definition.

C—Closest   O—Opposite or Nearly Opposite

1. Better yet, she was <u>on the verge of</u> cashing her first big paycheck.

_____ a. far from

_____ b. close to

_____ c. excited about

2. She was still <u>in a daze</u> and not quite sure what to do.

_____ a. confused

_____ b. surprised

_____ c. calm

3. Then she <u>slumped to</u> the floor.

_____ a. sat on

_____ b. rose from

_____ c. fell to

4. The shooting had been a <u>bizarre</u> accident.

_____ a. ordinary

_____ b. strange

_____ c. terrible

5. But she grew more <u>stable</u> with each passing minute.

_____ a. awake

_____ b. strong

_____ c. weak

_____ Score 3 points for each correct C answer.

_____ Score 2 points for each correct O answer.

_____ **Total Score:** Using Words Precisely

Enter the four total scores in the spaces below, and add them together to find your Reading Comprehension Score. Then record your score on the graph on page 57.

Score	Question Type	Lesson 3
_____	Finding the Main Idea	
_____	Recalling Facts	
_____	Making Inferences	
_____	Using Words Precisely	
_____	**Reading Comprehension Score**	

Author's Approach

Put an X in the box next to the correct answer.

1. The main purpose of the first paragraph is to

☐ a. introduce Kim Williams.

☐ b. give background information about the story.

☐ c. describe Kim Williams's golf game.

2. Which of the following statements from the article best describes Kim Williams's golf game before July 1994?

☐ a. At the Youngstown-Warren Classic she turned her game around.

☐ b. Until this point, she had not had much luck.

☐ c. Williams had not won a single tournament. In fact, she had never come close.

3. What do the authors imply by saying, "She felt poised to win for the first time"?

☐ a. Something would happen to keep her from winning.

☐ b. She had not felt as though she could win in previous tournaments.

☐ c. Williams wanted to win.

_____ Number of correct answers

Record your personal assessment of your work on the Critical Thinking Chart on page 58.

Summarizing and Paraphrasing

Follow the directions provided for questions 1 and 2. Put an X in the box next to the correct answer for question 3.

1. Look for the important ideas and events in paragraphs 7 and 8. Summarize those paragraphs in one or two sentences.

_____

_____

_____

_____

2. Complete the following one-sentence summary of the article using the lettered phrases from the phrase bank below. Write the letters on the lines.

> **Phrase bank:**
> a. a description of her golf career
> b. how she was shot
> c. an account of the tournament she played in right after being shot

The article about Kim Williams begins with _____, goes on

to explain _____, and ends with _____.

3. Choose the sentence that correctly restates the following sentence from the article: "Her chips and putts were right on the mark."

☐ a. Her chips and putts were exactly where she wanted them to be.

☐ b. Her chips and putts went right into the hole every time.

☐ c. Her chips and putts were going to the right of the hole.

> _____ Number of correct answers
>
> Record your personal assessment of your work on the Critical Thinking Chart on page 58.

Critical Thinking

Follow the directions provided for questions 1, 3, and 5. Put an X in the box next to the correct answer for questions 2 and 4.

1. For each statement below, write *O* if it expresses an opinion or *F* if it expresses a fact.

_____ a. For once, she felt as if she could beat anyone.

_____ b. Williams had not won a single tournament.

_____ c. Later she said she could feel the bullet every time she swallowed.

2. From the information in the article, you can predict that Williams

☐ a. eventually had the bullet removed.

☐ b. became a champion golfer.

☐ c. continued to play golf.

3. In which paragraph did you find the information or details to answer question 2?

_____

4. Choose from the letters below to correctly complete the following statement. Write the letters on the lines.

According to paragraph 12, _____ because _____.

a. they thought it was too risky

b. the doctors didn't take the bullet out

c. it hadn't hit any organs

5. What did you have to do to answer question 4?

☐ a. find an opinion (what someone thinks about something)

☐ b. find a purpose (why something is done)

☐ c. find an effect (something that happened)

_____ Number of correct answers

Record your personal assessment of your work on the Critical Thinking Chart on page 58.

Personal Response

What was most surprising or interesting to you about this article?

_____

_____

_____

_____

Self-Assessment

From reading this article, I have learned

_____

_____

_____

_____

Trapped on the 37th Floor

The 1988 fire in the First Interstate Bank building was the worst high-rise fire in Los Angeles's history.

Melinda Skaar wasn't expecting any phone calls. Skaar was working late in her office at the First Interstate Bank of California. By 10:45 that night—May 4, 1988—she was almost ready to go home. That's when the phone rang.

2   Picking it up, she heard a security guard on the other end of the line. "There's a fire!" he shouted. "Get out of there!"

3   Skaar didn't panic. She figured that it was just a small blaze elsewhere in the building. Her office building was huge. There were 62 floors in the First

Interstate Tower. Skaar's desk was on the 37th floor.

4   Skaar called out to office mate Stephen Oksas, who had also stayed late to work. The two of them headed for the hallway. But when they got there, they were met by a cloud of black smoke. They rushed back into the main office. Slamming the door, Skaar took off her jacket. She stuffed it into the crack at the bottom of the door. She hoped that would keep the smoke from seeping in.

5   Then she and Oksas turned to the phone. They called 911 and reported that they were trapped. Before they could call their families, however, the line went dead. That meant that they were completely cut off from the outside world. All they could do was wait and hope someone would come to rescue them.

6   Skaar and Oksas didn't know it, but they were caught in the worst high-rise fire in Los Angeles's history. The blaze began on the 12th floor. From there, it spread quickly to the next four levels. Temperatures on those floors rose to 2,000 degrees. The air was so hot that it melted metal. It blew out windows. It also melted the glue that held the carpets in place. The burning glue filled the air with black, toxic fumes.

7   The giant blaze could be seen for miles around. Three hundred fire-fighters were called in. Most had never seen anything like it before. They struggled bravely, but the fire kept spreading. Firefighters knew that if it got past the 16th floor, the whole building might collapse.

8   Meanwhile, up on the 37th floor, Skaar and Oksas waited. The minutes ticked by. Smoke began to waft into the office. It billowed up the stairwells and through the air vents. Soon it became hard for Skaar and Oksas to breathe.

9   They thought about trying to run down the 37 flights of stairs. Or they could head up the remaining flights to the roof. But they didn't think they could make it. They would probably die from smoke inhalation before they even got close to safety.

10   Looking around, they spotted a small workroom. It seemed to have cleaner air. So Skaar and Oksas huddled in there. "We found these . . . water bottles in there and cut holes in the bottom," Skaar later recalled. "Then we put paper towels over the holes to filter the air and we breathed through those."

11   That helped for a while, but in time even the workroom was filled with deadly smoke. The bottles weren't much good then. Skaar and Oksas did everything they could to find fresh air. They went to a cupboard in the corner of the room. Every once in a while they opened the door. They took a deep breath of clean air and then quickly closed the door again.

12   Oksas and Skaar knew they were running out of time. Desperate, they tried to break one of the outside windows, but the glass was not breakable. It was sealed with a heavy rubber coating. Oksas picked up a table. He threw it at a window. It just bounced back. Together, he and Skaar picked up an empty file cabinet. They flung it at the window. It, too, bounced to the floor. They tried other windows, but the same thing happened. They picked up other cabinets and threw those. "They just

bounced back," said Skaar. "Everything just bounced back."

13   At last, Skaar grabbed a pair of scissors. She tried to scrape away the rubber coating at the edge of the window. She worked and worked. She managed to let in a tiny hair-thin trickle of air. That was it. It didn't provide enough oxygen for even a single breath.

14   Defeated, Skaar and Oksas staggered back to the workroom. They felt weak and dizzy. Shortly after that, Skaar heard a helicopter outside. "I thought I had to wave to them, to let them know we were still alive," she said. So she left Oksas and stumbled back out to the main room. She waved at the helicopter, but she didn't have much hope. She didn't think rescuers could ever reach her in time.

15   "I thought, I'm definitely [going] to die in this," she said. "I thought about all the things that would go unfinished in my life. How people would find us, here, on the floor . . . I thought about my parents, about my family . . . "

16   After she felt her way back to the workroom, she found that Oksas had passed out. Skaar knew she couldn't hang on much longer, either. By this time, she could barely walk. She shuffled over to the window where the tiny trickle of air was drifting in. Then she, too, collapsed.

17   As Skaar and Oksas lay near death, rescuers were rushing to find them. It had taken three and a half hours, but firefighters had finally brought the fire under control. By 2:15 A.M. they had beaten it back. Soon after, they found the body of one man who had died in an elevator. They rescued several people from the roof and one man from the 50th floor. The only ones left to be found were Skaar and Oksas.

18   At last, at about 4 A.M., firefighters reached the 37th floor. There they saw Oksas and Skaar. "All I remember is seeing these bodies . . . " said Skaar. "Strong bodies that weren't like ours, bodies that could walk and breathe and had equipment with them and would rescue us."

19   The firefighters pulled curtains off the windows and used them as stretchers. Then they hurried Skaar and Oksas outside. Both were rushed to the hospital.

20   Melinda Skaar and Stephen Oksas knew they were lucky to be alive. "Sunday's my birthday," Skaar told one reporter the next day. She would be turning 29. But she knew that she had already gotten the best present possible—the gift of life.

If you have been timed while reading this article, enter your reading time below. Then turn to the Words-per-Minute Table on page 55 and look up your reading speed (words per minute). Enter your reading speed on the graph on page 56.

Reading Time: Lesson 4

_____ : _____
Minutes   Seconds

A Finding the Main Idea

One statement below expresses the main idea of the article. One statement is too general, or too broad. The other statement explains only part of the article; it is too narrow. Label the statements using the following key:

M—Main Idea   **B—Too Broad**   **N—Too Narrow**

_____ 1. When they realized they were trapped in the burning building, Melinda Skaar and Stephen Oksas hid in a small workroom.

_____ 2. In May 1988 a dangerous fire broke out in the First Interstate Bank building, one of the tallest high-rises in Los Angeles.

_____ 3. On the night of May 4, 1988, a fire broke out in the First Interstate Bank building in Los Angeles, nearly killing several people who were in the building at the time.

_____ Score 15 points for a correct M answer.

_____ Score 5 points for each correct B or N answer.

_____ **Total Score:** Finding the Main Idea

B Recalling Facts

How well do you remember the facts in the article? Put an X in the box next to the answer that correctly completes each statement about the article.

1. When Skaar and Oksas heard there was a fire in the building, they
   ☐ a. called 911 to report that they were trapped.
   ☐ b. tried to run down the stairs.
   ☐ c. immediately ran to a small workroom to hide.

2. The fire in the First Interstate building
   ☐ a. spread to 12 floors.
   ☐ b. was the worst high-rise fire in Los Angeles's history.
   ☐ c. melted the glass in the building.

3. Skaar and Oksas were able to breathe fresh air
   ☐ a. through a small crack in a window.
   ☐ b. through paper towels.
   ☐ c. from a cupboard in the workroom.

4. Skaar and Oksas were rescued
   ☐ a. just before they passed out.
   ☐ b. $3\frac{1}{2}$ hours after the fire started.
   ☐ c. last of all the people in the building.

5. Skaar and Oksas were
   ☐ a. carried out of the building on curtains.
   ☐ b. carried to the hospital by helicopter.
   ☐ c. found too late.

Score 5 points for each correct answer.

_____ **Total Score:** Recalling Facts

Making Inferences

When you combine your own experience with information from a text to draw a conclusion that is not directly stated in that text, you are making an inference. Below are five statements that may or may not be inferences based on information in the article. Label the statements using the following key:

C—Correct Inference   F—Faulty Inference

_____ 1. Smoke from the fire had spread throughout the whole building.

_____ 2. Skaar and Oksas had been caught in fires before.

_____ 3. The city of Los Angeles employs more than 300 firefighters.

_____ 4. The First Interstate Bank building did not have a sprinkler system.

_____ 5. There were a lot of people in the First Interstate Bank building when the fire broke out.

Score 5 points for each correct answer.

_____ **Total Score:** Making Inferences

D **Using Words Precisely**

Each numbered sentence below contains an underlined word or phrase from the article. Following the sentence are three definitions. One definition is closest to the meaning of the underlined word. One definition is opposite or nearly opposite. Label those two definitions using the following key; do not label the remaining definition.

C—Closest   O—Opposite or Nearly Opposite

1. The burning glue filled the air with black, <u>toxic</u> fumes.

_____ a. smelly

_____ b. harmless

_____ c. poisonous

2. Smoke began to <u>waft</u> into the office.

_____ a. drift

_____ b. rise

_____ c. rush

3. So Skaar and Oksas <u>huddled</u> in there.

_____ a. stretched out

_____ b. crowded together

_____ c. made plans

4. <u>Desperate</u>, they tried to break one of the outside windows.

_____ a. Forcefully

_____ b. Hopelessly

_____ c. Calmly

5. It didn't <u>provide</u> enough oxygen for even a single breath.

_____ a. take

_____ b. refuse

_____ c. supply

_____ Score 3 points for each correct C answer.

_____ Score 2 points for each correct O answer.

_____ **Total Score:** Using Words Precisely

Enter the four total scores in the spaces below, and add them together to find your Reading Comprehension Score. Then record your score on the graph on page 57.

Score	Question Type	Lesson 4
_____	Finding the Main Idea	
_____	Recalling Facts	
_____	Making Inferences	
_____	Using Words Precisely	
_____	**Reading Comprehension Score**	

Author's Approach

Put an X in the box next to the correct answer.

1. The authors use the first sentence of the article to

☐ a. describe Melinda Skaar.

☐ b. get the reader's attention.

☐ c. entertain the reader.

2. What is the authors' purpose in writing "Trapped on the 37th Floor"?

☐ a. to express an opinion about the rescue operation

☐ b. to warn the reader about the dangers of high-rise buildings

☐ c. to inform the reader about the fire

3. The authors tell this story mainly by

☐ a. retelling personal experiences of the people involved.

☐ b. telling different stories about the same topic.

☐ c. using their imagination and creativity.

_____ Number of correct answers

Record your personal assessment of your work on the Critical Thinking Chart on page 58.

Summarizing and Paraphrasing

Follow the directions provided for question 1. Put an X in the box next to the correct answer for questions 2 and 3.

1. Reread paragraph 12 in the article. Below, write a summary of the paragraph in no more than 25 words.

_____

_____

_____

_____

Reread your summary and decide whether it covers the important ideas in the paragraph. Next, decide how to shorten the summary to 15 words or less without leaving out any essential information. Write this summary below.

_____

_____

_____

2. Below are summaries of the article. Choose the summary that says all the most important things about the article but in the fewest words.

☐ a. The fire that started in the First Interstate Bank building in Los Angeles in May 1988 was the worst high-rise fire in the city's history.

☐ b. The fire that started in the First Interstate Bank building in Los Angeles burned for over three hours and trapped several people, including Melinda Skaar and Stephen Oksas, who worked on the 37th floor and had stayed late in the office.

☐ c. The First Interstate Bank building caught on fire in May 1988, trapping several people for over three hours, including office workers Melinda Skaar and Stephen Oksas.

3. Read the statement from the article below. Then read the paraphrase of that statement. Choose the reason that best tells why the paraphrase does not say the same thing as the statement.

Statement: "She figured that it was just a small blaze elsewhere in the building."

Paraphrase: She thought that the fire had started in another part of the building.

☐ a. Paraphrase says too much.

☐ b. Paraphrase doesn't say enough.

☐ c. Paraphrase doesn't agree with the statement from the article.

_____ Number of correct answers

Record your personal assessment of your work on the Critical Thinking Chart on page 58.

Critical Thinking

Put an X in the box next to the correct answer for questions 1, 2, and 4. Follow the directions provided for questions 3 and 5.

1. Which of the following statements from the article is an opinion rather than a fact?

   ☐ a. The giant blaze could be seen for miles around.

   ☐ b. They would probably die from smoke inhalation before they even got close to safety.

   ☐ c. She managed to let in a tiny hair-thin trickle of air.

2. Based on Melinda Skaar's actions in this article, you can conclude that she

   ☐ a. remains calm under pressure.

   ☐ b. was trained as a firefighter.

   ☐ c. quit her job at First Interstate Bank after the fire.

3. Choose from the letters below to correctly complete the following statement. Write the letters on the lines.

   On the positive side, _____, but on the negative side _____.

   a. the blaze killed one man

   b. Melinda Skaar and Stephen Oksas survived the fire

   c. it was the biggest high-rise fire in Los Angeles's history

4. What was the effect of Skaar and Oksas's huddling in the workroom?

   ☐ a. They began to run out of fresh air.

   ☐ b. They were able to stay conscious longer.

   ☐ c. They breathed fresh air from a cupboard in the room.

5. Which paragraphs provide evidence to support your answer to question 4?

_____

_____

_____ Number of correct answers

Record your personal assessment of your work on the Critical Thinking Chart on page 58.

Personal Response

What would you have done if you were in the building when the fire broke out?

_____

_____

_____

Self-Assessment

When reading the article, I was having trouble with

_____

_____

_____

Near Death on the Football Field

It would be the last game of the year for one team or the other. Would it be the New York Jets or the Detroit Lions? The winning team would go on to the National Football League playoffs. The losing team would be finished for the season. So there was a great deal at stake when the Jets and the Lions met in Detroit on December 21, 1997. Before the end of the day, though, there would be much more on the line than just a football game.

Reggie Brown makes a play during a game. This photo was taken before a spinal cord injury forced Brown to give up his career as a football player.

2   For three quarters, the game hung in the balance. Fans on both sides screamed and yelled on every play. Then, all of a sudden, the fans fell silent. They saw a player lying still on the field. It was Reggie Brown, a linebacker for the Lions. Brown had just tackled one of the Jets. But his helmet had hit the other man at a weird angle. As the rest of the players got up from the pile, Brown didn't move.

3   Luther Elliss, a Lion, offered his hand to help his teammate up. "Let's go," he said.

4   But Brown still didn't react. He didn't move. "He just kind of mouthed the words, 'I can't get up,'" said Elliss.

5   Lions trainer Kent Falb rushed onto the field. Kneeling by Brown's side, he saw right away that Brown was in trouble. "Dear God," he mumbled. "Don't let me lose another one." For a moment, Falb's mind flashed back to 1971. He had been on the field when Detroit Lion Chuck Hughes had died from a heart attack. Falb had also been there in 1991 when Lion Mike Utley had hurt his spine. Utley was never able to walk again.

6   Team doctor Terry Lock ran onto the field to join Falb. By this time Brown wasn't even breathing. His lips were turning blue. He had no pulse. To Falb and Lock it looked like a spinal injury. They knew they had to do something and do it fast.

7   Players on both sides crowded around. They, too, realized that Brown had suffered a serious injury. Some had tears in their eyes. Others went down on their knees to pray. Some of the players cried out for help. Lion Herman Moore couldn't bear to look. "It is a situation that you know can happen, but you don't believe it will," Moore said. "It seemed unreal. We take for granted when we hit the ground we're going to get back up."

8   The game was being broadcast on national TV, so millions of fans at home also saw Brown go down. One viewer was his mother. She usually didn't worry about her son getting hurt. So when the announcer said it was Brown on the field, she thought, "No, that can't be Reggie. There must be some mistake." Then she realized it was indeed her son lying there immobile. "I just dropped to my knees," she said, "and started praying."

9   Without breathing, Brown had only a few minutes to live. In most cases, doctors are careful not to move the neck of a person who has hurt his spine. But Falb and Lock felt they had no choice. They had to get Brown's helmet off. That was the only way they could begin mouth-to-mouth resuscitation. So Falb lifted Brown's head and put his hand behind his neck. One false move and Brown would die in his arms. Gently, Lock slipped off the helmet.

10   Then Lock began to blow air into Brown's lungs. It worked. Brown's chest began to go up and down again. Soon he began breathing on his own. His pulse also came back. For the moment, at least, he was alive.

11   Carefully Brown was put on a special board to support his neck. By that time, he had been lying on the field for 17 minutes. To those who saw it, it seemed more like 17 hours. At last an ambulance came and took Brown to the hospital. Falb and Lock had done their best. But would it be enough? It looked like Brown would

survive. But would he, like Utley, be unable to walk again?

12   The odds of a full recovery were not good. Doctors say that half of all people with this type of spinal cord injury never walk again. But the 23-year-old Brown was lucky. Except for the injury, he was a strong, healthy young man. He was helped by the quick work of Trainer Kent Falb and Doctor Terry Lock. In addition, the doctors were able to use a brand new treatment on Brown. Six months earlier this treatment would not have been available.

13   Brown had a powerful drive to get well. From the start, he was determined to walk again. He had a lot of people pulling for him. Herman Moore showed him a video. It was filled with get-well messages from the Detroit Lions. Brown also got a letter from Mike Utley. It read: "Dear Reggie: Don't give up. Don't ever quit."

14   Reggie didn't quit. And soon he was back on his feet. He was shaky at first, but he got stronger with each day. Doctors didn't want him to move his neck or head for three months. So he wore a brace called a "halo" on his head. He wasn't as strong as he had been. His arms and feet often felt a bit numb. Still, his doctors couldn't believe how fast he recovered. "I've never seen anyone else come so far so fast," said one.

15   So Brown considered himself a lucky man. He was later asked what he felt just before he blacked out on the field. Brown said that he thought for sure he was going to die. "I was thinking, 'I'm too young. I never had the chance to get married. I never had the chance to have kids. I never did this, I never did that.' It is a strange feeling when you know you are going to die."

16   Reggie Brown will never play football again. And he can't do things that might hurt his head or neck. But he can do everything else. After leaving the hospital, he was asked about what he would do. "I want to do a lot of things," he said. "I'll never play football again. I'm sorry about that. But this is just God's way of sending me down another avenue in life."

If you have been timed while reading this article, enter your reading time below. Then turn to the Words-per-Minute Table on page 55 and look up your reading speed (words per minute). Enter your reading speed on the graph on page 56.

Reading Time: Lesson 5

_____ : _____
Minutes   Seconds

A Finding the Main Idea

One statement below expresses the main idea of the article. One statement is too general, or too broad. The other statement explains only part of the article; it is too narrow. Label the statements using the following key:

M—Main Idea   **B—Too Broad**   **N—Too Narrow**

_____ 1. No one thought that Reggie Brown would walk again after being injured on the football field, but he surprised everyone with his quick recovery.

_____ 2. According to doctors, half of the people with a spinal cord injury like Reggie Brown's never walk again.

_____ 3. Reggie Brown injured his spinal cord during a football game in 1997.

_____ Score 15 points for a correct M answer.

_____ Score 5 points for each correct B or N answer.

_____ **Total Score:** Finding the Main Idea

B Recalling Facts

How well do you remember the facts in the article? Put an X in the box next to the answer that correctly completes each statement about the article.

1. Reggie Brown was injured
   ☐ a. when another player hit him at a weird angle.
   ☐ b. while tackling one of the Jets.
   ☐ c. while playing against the Detroit Lions.

2. When team doctor Terry Lock rushed onto the field,
   ☐ a. he had tears in his eyes.
   ☐ b. Brown wasn't even breathing.
   ☐ c. Brown was having a heart attack.

3. Falb and Lock moved Brown's neck because it
   ☐ a. was the only way they could revive him.
   ☐ b. helps a person who has hurt his or her spine.
   ☐ c. would help him to breathe.

4. A new treatment for spinal cord injuries
   ☐ a. became available six months after Brown's injury.
   ☐ b. helped Brown to recover quickly.
   ☐ c. made Brown's hands and feet numb.

5. When Brown was down on the field, he
   ☐ a. thought he was going to die.
   ☐ b. regretted things he had done in his life.
   ☐ c. thought about his wife and kids.

Score 5 points for each correct answer.

_____ **Total Score:** Recalling Facts

C Making Inferences

When you combine your own experience with information from a text to draw a conclusion that is not directly stated in that text, you are making an inference. Below are five statements that may or may not be inferences based on information in the article. Label the statements using the following key:

C—Correct Inference   F—Faulty Inference

_____ 1. Having no pulse indicates that a person has a spinal injury.

_____ 2. It is dangerous to move the neck of someone with a spinal injury.

_____ 3. The spinal cord affects a person's ability to walk.

_____ 4. Reggie Brown will become a soccer player.

_____ 5. The support he received from friends and family helped Brown to recover more quickly.

Score 5 points for each correct answer.

_____ **Total Score:** Making Inferences

D Using Words Precisely

Each numbered sentence below contains an underlined word or phrase from the article. Following the sentence are three definitions. One definition is closest to the meaning of the underlined word. One definition is opposite or nearly opposite. Label those two definitions using the following key; do not label the remaining definition.

C—Closest   O—Opposite or Nearly Opposite

1. Then she realized it was indeed her son lying there <u>immobile</u>.

_____ a. curled up

_____ b. still

_____ c. moving

2. Carefully Brown was put on a special board to <u>support</u> his neck.

_____ a. hold up

_____ b. drop

_____ c. straighten

3. Brown had a powerful <u>drive</u> to get well.

_____ a. lack of interest

_____ b. desire

_____ c. force

4. Still, his doctors couldn't believe how fast he <u>recovered</u>.

_____ a. walked

_____ b. got worse

_____ c. got better

5. He was later asked what he felt just before he <u>blacked out</u> on the field.

_____ a. passed out

_____ b. fell down

_____ c. came to

_____ Score 3 points for each correct C answer.

_____ Score 2 points for each correct O answer.

_____ **Total Score:** Using Words Precisely

Enter the four total scores in the spaces below, and add them together to find your Reading Comprehension Score. Then record your score on the graph on page 57.

Score	Question Type	Lesson 5
_____	Finding the Main Idea	
_____	Recalling Facts	
_____	Making Inferences	
_____	Using Words Precisely	
_____	**Reading Comprehension Score**	

Author's Approach

Put an X in the box next to the correct answer.

1. The main purpose of the first paragraph is to

☐ a. describe the setting of the story.

☐ b. describe the game in which Reggie Brown was injured.

☐ c. introduce Reggie Brown.

2. What do the authors mean by the statement, "Before the end of the day, though, there would be much more on the line than just a football game"?

☐ a. Before the end of the day, the football players would be lined up on the field.

☐ b. By the end of the day, the outcome of the football game would not seem so important.

☐ c. By the end of the day the football game would be over.

3. The authors probably wrote this article to

☐ a. make people aware of the dangers of playing football.

☐ b. tell Reggie Brown's inspiring story.

☐ c. inform people about spinal injuries.

_____ Number of correct answers

Record your personal assessment of your work on the Critical Thinking Chart on page 58.

Summarizing and Paraphrasing

Follow the directions provided for questions 1 and 2. Put an X in the box next to the correct answer for question 3.

1. Look for the important ideas and events in paragraphs 9 and 10. Summarize those paragraphs in one or two sentences.

_____

_____

_____

2. Complete the following one-sentence summary of the article using the lettered phrases from the phrase bank below. Write the letters on the lines.

Phrase bank:
a. his treatment and recovery
b. Brown discussing his experiences
c. a description of how he was hurt

The article about Reggie Brown begins with _____, goes

on to explain _____, and ends with _____.

3. Choose the sentence that correctly restates the following sentence from the article: "The odds of a full recovery are not good."

☐ a. It is not likely that Brown will recover.

☐ b. It would be odd for Brown to recover.

☐ c. The chances of recovering completely are not good.

_____ Number of correct answers

Record your personal assessment of your work on the Critical Thinking Chart on page 58.

Critical Thinking

Follow the directions provided for questions 1, 3, and 4. Put an X in the box next to the correct answer for questions 2 and 5.

1. For each statement below, write O if it expresses an opinion or F if it expresses a fact.

_____ a. To Falb and Lock it looked like a spinal injury.

_____ b. Brown's chest began to go up and down again.

_____ c. Brown said that he thought for sure he was going to die.

2. From the information in the article, you can predict that Reggie Brown will

☐ a. live a normal life.

☐ b. always have difficulty walking.

☐ c. become a football coach.

3. Which paragraphs provide evidence from the article to support your answer to question 2?

_____

4. Choose from the letters below to correctly complete the following statement. Write the letters on the lines.

According to paragraph 2, _____ because _____.

a. he had tackled one of the Jets

b. his helmet had hit another player at a strange angle

c. Reggie Brown could not get up

5. What did you have to do to answer question 4?

☐ a. find a purpose (why something is done)

☐ b. find a cause (why something happened)

☐ c. find a contrast (how things are different)

_____ Number of correct answers

Record your personal assessment of your work on the Critical Thinking Chart on page 58.

Personal Response

I can't believe

_____

_____

_____

_____

Self-Assessment

A word or phrase in the article that I do not understand is

_____

_____

_____

_____

Compare and Contrast

Think about the articles you have read in Unit One. Pick the three articles you thought included the most frightening situations. Write the titles of the articles in the first column of the chart below. Use information you have learned from the articles to fill in the empty boxes in the chart.

Title	Why would you have been frightened in this situation?	What would you have done if you had been the main character in this article?	What person in this article do you think is brave? Why do you think this?

Which of these situations would you least like to have been in? Why?

_____

_____

Words-per-Minute Table

Unit One

Directions: If you were timed while reading an article, refer to the Reading Time you recorded in the box at the end of the article. Use this words-per-minute table to determine your reading speed for that article. Then plot your reading speed on the graph on page 56.

Lesson No. of Words	Sample 713	1 1266	2 995	3 1015	4 1080	5 1062	
1:30	475	844	663	677	720	708	**90**
1:40	428	760	597	609	648	637	**100**
1:50	389	691	543	554	589	579	**110**
2:00	357	633	498	508	540	531	**120**
2:10	329	584	459	468	498	490	**130**
2:20	306	543	426	435	463	455	**140**
2:30	285	506	398	406	432	425	**150**
2:40	267	475	373	381	405	398	**160**
2:50	252	447	351	358	381	375	**170**
3:00	238	422	332	338	360	354	**180**
3:10	225	400	314	321	341	335	**190**
3:20	214	380	299	305	324	319	**200**
3:30	204	362	284	290	309	303	**210**
3:40	194	345	271	277	295	290	**220**
3:50	186	330	260	265	282	277	**230**
4:00	178	317	249	254	270	266	**240**
4:10	171	304	239	244	259	255	**250**
4:20	165	292	230	234	249	245	**260**
4:30	158	281	221	226	240	236	**270**
4:40	153	271	213	218	231	228	**280**
4:50	148	262	206	210	223	220	**290**
5:00	143	253	199	203	216	212	**300**
5:10	138	245	193	196	209	206	**310**
5:20	134	237	187	190	203	199	**320**
5:30	130	230	181	185	196	193	**330**
5:40	126	223	176	179	191	187	**340**
5:50	122	217	171	174	185	182	**350**
6:00	119	211	166	169	180	177	**360**
6:10	116	205	161	165	175	172	**370**
6:20	113	200	157	160	171	168	**380**
6:30	110	195	153	156	166	163	**390**
6:40	107	190	149	152	162	159	**400**
6:50	104	185	146	149	158	155	**410**
7:00	102	181	142	145	154	152	**420**
7:10	99	177	139	142	151	148	**430**
7:20	97	173	136	138	147	145	**440**
7:30	95	169	133	135	144	142	**450**
7:40	93	165	130	132	141	139	**460**
7:50	91	162	127	130	138	136	**470**
8:00	89	158	124	127	135	133	**480**

Minutes and Seconds

Seconds

Plotting Your Progress: Reading Speed

Unit One

Directions: If you were timed while reading an article, write your words-per-minute rate for that article in the box under the number of the lesson. Then plot your reading speed on the graph by putting a small X on the line directly above the number of the lesson, across from the number of words per minute you read. As you mark your speed for each lesson, graph your progress by drawing a line to connect the X's.

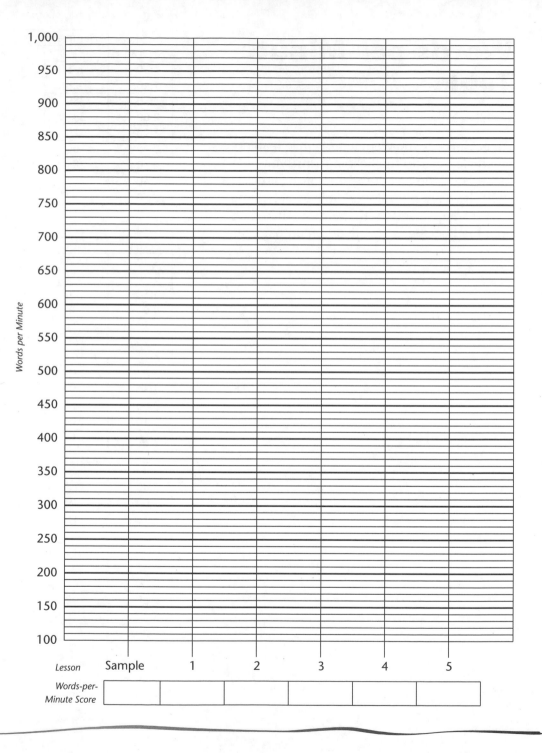

Lesson	Sample	1	2	3	4	5
Words-per-Minute Score						

Plotting Your Progress: Reading Comprehension

Unit One

Directions: Write your Reading Comprehension score for each lesson in the box under the number of the lesson. Then plot your score on the graph by putting a small X on the line directly above the number of the lesson and across from the score you earned. As you mark your score for each lesson, graph your progress by drawing a line to connect the X's.

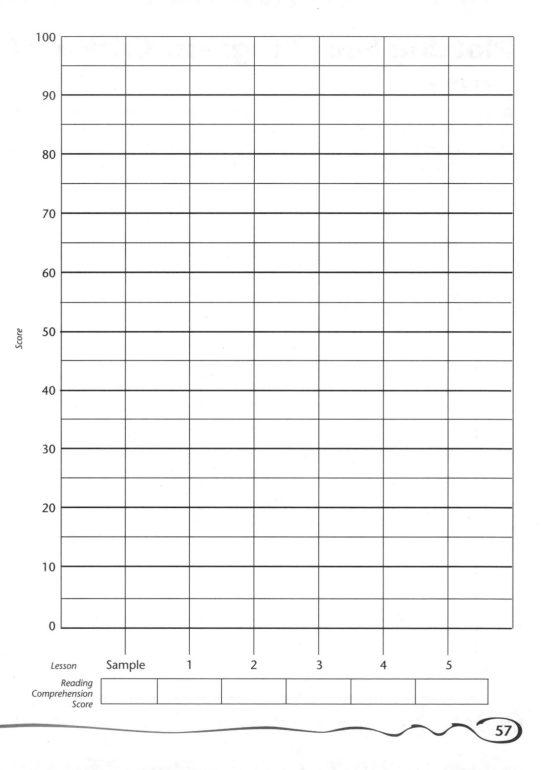

Score

Lesson	Sample	1	2	3	4	5
Reading Comprehension Score						

Plotting Your Progress: Critical Thinking

Unit One

Directions: Work with your teacher to evaluate your responses to the Critical Thinking questions for each lesson. Then fill in the appropriate spaces in the chart below. For each lesson and each type of Critical Thinking question, do the following: Mark a minus sign (–) in the box to indicate areas in which you feel you could improve. Mark a plus sign (+) to indicate areas in which you feel you did well. Mark a minus-slash-plus sign (–/+) to indicate areas in which you had mixed success. Then write any comments you have about your performance, including ideas for improvement.

Lesson	Author's Approach	Summarizing and Paraphrasing	Critical Thinking
Sample			
1			
2			
3			
4			
5			

UNIT TWO

Desert Disaster

The bleak landscape of the Takla Makan desert is similar to that of the Sahara Desert, shown here. Explorer Sven Hedin barely survived a trek across the Takla Makan in 1895.

The local people cried when they heard Sven Hedin's plans. They couldn't believe he was going off into the Mankiller Desert. The desert's real name was Takla Makan, but most people in western China just called it the Mankiller. They said that evil spirits lurked in this vast stretch of sand. They said that the spirits led travelers astray and then left them to die.

2   Hedin did not believe the stories. Still, the Swedish explorer felt a strong pull to investigate this Asian desert. As he wrote, "I had fallen

under the spell of the weird witchcraft of the desert." For him, the biggest thrill would be walking where no human had ever walked before. "I knew that beyond the sand dunes, amid the grave-like silence, stretched the unknown, enchanted land . . . " It was "land that I was going to be the first to tread."

3   And so, in April of 1895, Hedin set out. With him went a servant named Islam Bai. This man had traveled with Hedin on several previous expeditions. Three local men had also agreed to go. One was a scout named Yollchi. He had been into the desert before in search of gold. He claimed that he could get Hedin across it with no trouble. The group took eight strong camels, each packed with water casks, food, and other supplies.

4   At first, the journey went well. On the third day the group came across a spring. Happily they refilled their water casks. By the sixth day they had gone more than 50 miles. "We were getting farther and farther into the unknown ocean of sandy desert," wrote Hedin. "Not a sign of life to be seen, not a sound to be heard . . . "

5   On the tenth day, April 20, the group came to an oasis. Here they found pools of water and thick green grass. Yollchi told Hedin that they were near the Khotan River. He said that they should reach it within four days. Once they got there, they would have all the water they needed for the rest of the trip.

6   Hedin was thrilled. It seemed that they would make it to the eastern end of the desert without difficulty. He even decided to give the camels a break. He ordered the water casks filled just halfway to the top. That would ease the burden on the tired animals, and it would still be more than enough for the group. Hedin figured half-full casks would last them 10 days.

7   Unfortunately, Yollchi was wrong. The Khotan River was not four days away. It was a full 15 days' journey from where the men stood. On April 24 Hedin and his men ran into a terrible sandstorm. "Clouds and columns of sand whirled in a mad dance across the desert," he wrote. "The fine red drift-sand penetrated everywhere—into mouth, nose, ears . . . "

8   The next day Hedin discovered that they were almost out of water. It turned out that the servants hadn't filled the water casks all the way to the halfway mark. Grimly, Hedin cut everyone's water rations way down. The group dug deep into the sand, looking for a well or a spring, but they found nothing. Knowing they couldn't properly water eight thirsty camels, they decided to leave two behind. Then they hurried on through the hot, dusty desert, hoping to reach the Khotan River soon.

9   By April 30 they were in real trouble. It had been 10 days since they left had the oasis. They were now totally out of water. They had also dumped most of their food to lighten their load. "We are all terribly weak, men as well as camels," wrote Hedin in his diary that day. "God help us all!"

10   The next day brought another endless walk through the scorching heat. Hedin kept scanning the horizon, but he saw no sign of the Khotan River. One of the men became convinced that evil spirits had led them in the wrong direction. All of

them were growing nervous. They were no longer sure they would get out of this desert alive.

11   Later that day they couldn't stand their thirst any longer. They decided to drink some strong Chinese brandy, which they had been using to fuel their stove. The strong drink made them all sick. It even killed one of the men.

12   By May 3 most of the camels were dead, and Yollchi had disappeared. Somewhere on the long, hot march he had fallen behind and now he had completely dropped out of sight. Neither Hedin nor the others had the strength to turn back for him. That same day, Islam Bai collapsed. He was too weak to walk. Hedin was heartbroken, but he had no choice. He left Islam Bai with the last camel and a few provisions. Then he and his remaining servant, Kasim, stumbled on alone.

13   Finally, on May 5, Hedin glimpsed trees in the distance. That meant there was water up ahead. Leaving Kasim to rest, Hedin dragged himself through the blazing sun toward the trees. When he reached them, he sank down next to the Khotan River. He drank and drank until he could drink no more. Then he took off his boots and filled them with water. Carefully he carried them back to Kasim so he, too, could have a drink.

14   For Hedin, the worst was over. Now that he had water, his strength returned. The next day he and Kasim met some shepherds who gave them food and shelter. Four days after that he and Kasim were resting by the bank of the Khotan River. In the distance he saw another group of shepherds walking toward them. To Hedin's joy, these shepherds had Islam Bai with them!

15   When Islam Bai reached Hedin, he explained that the shepherds had found him as he lay in the sand. They had given him food and water. They had also rescued his camel. In the camel's bags were Hedin's diary and maps, so the record of the group's journey was saved.

16   A few days later Sven Hedin, Islam Bai, and Kasim at last walked out of the desert. They had done what they set out to do. They had crossed Takla Makan, the Mankiller desert. But two people and seven camels had died along the way. And even for those who survived, it had been a very grim journey indeed.

If you have been timed while reading this article, enter your reading time below. Then turn to the Words-per-Minute Table on page 101 and look up your reading speed (words per minute). Enter your reading speed on the graph on page 102.

Reading Time: Lesson 6

_____ : _____
Minutes   Seconds

A Finding the Main Idea

One statement below expresses the main idea of the article. One statement is too general, or too broad. The other statement explains only part of the article; it is too narrow. Label the statements using the following key:

M—Main Idea   **B—Too Broad**   **N—Too Narrow**

_____ 1. Swedish explorer Sven Hedin set out to explore China's "Mankiller" desert in April of 1895.

_____ 2. On his trek across the Takla Makan desert, Sven Hedin had to leave two of his eight camels behind because the group was running out of water.

_____ 3. In 1895 Swedish explorer Sven Hedin became the first person to cross China's Takla Makan desert, running out of water and losing several of his group members and camels along the way.

_____ Score 15 points for a correct M answer.

_____ Score 5 points for each correct B or N answer.

_____ **Total Score:** Finding the Main Idea

B Recalling Facts

How well do you remember the facts in the article? Put an X in the box next to the answer that correctly completes each statement about the article.

1. Sven Hedin wanted to explore the Takla Makan desert because he wanted to
   ☐ a. see if the stories about evil spirits in the desert were true.
   ☐ b. walk where no human had walked before.
   ☐ c. study the desert.

2. After traveling for ten days, the group
   ☐ a. came to an oasis.
   ☐ b. was only four days away from the Khotan River.
   ☐ c. had gone 50 miles.

3. After Hedin's expedition ran out of water,
   ☐ a. evil spirits led them in the wrong direction.
   ☐ b. they were still 10 days away from the Khotan River.
   ☐ c. they drank Chinese brandy to quench their thirst, but it made them sick.

4. By the time Hedin reached the Khotan River,
   ☐ a. only he and one of his servants were strong enough to walk.
   ☐ b. only he and one of his servants were still alive.
   ☐ c. he had met some shepherds, who gave him food and water.

5. During Hedin's trip across the Takla Makan desert,
   ☐ a. he lost his diary and maps.
   ☐ b. two people and seven camels died.
   ☐ c. he had to give up his dream to reach the other side.

Score 5 points for each correct answer.

_____ **Total Score:** Recalling Facts

C | Making Inferences

When you combine your own experience with information from a text to draw a conclusion that is not directly stated in that text, you are making an inference. Below are five statements that may or may not be inferences based on information in the article. Label the statements using the following key:

C—Correct Inference   F—Faulty Inference

_____ 1. Most people were afraid to cross the Takla Makan desert.

_____ 2. The scout, Yollchi, had never really gone into the desert before his trip with Hedin.

_____ 3. Hedin's group set out carrying enough water for 20 days.

_____ 4. Camels can survive for weeks without water.

_____ 5. Shepherds lived in the Takla Makan desert.

Score 5 points for each correct answer.

_____ **Total Score:** Making Inferences

D | Using Words Precisely

Each numbered sentence below contains an underlined word or phrase from the article. Following the sentence are three definitions. One definition is closest to the meaning of the underlined word. One definition is opposite or nearly opposite. Label those two definitions using the following key; do not label the remaining definition.

C—Closest   O—Opposite or Nearly Opposite

1. They said the spirits led travelers <u>astray</u> and then left them to die.

_____ a. off course

_____ b. in the right direction

_____ c. away

2. That would <u>ease</u> the burden on the tired animals.

_____ a. increase

_____ b. remove

_____ c. lessen

3. "The fine red drift-sand <u>penetrated</u> everywhere—into mouth, nose, ears . . ."

_____ a. filled

_____ b. entered

_____ c. left

4. The next day brought another endless walk through the <u>scorching</u> heat.

_____ a. burning

_____ b. dry

_____ c. freezing

5. And even for those who survived, it had been a very <u>grim</u> journey indeed.

_____ a. long

_____ b. pleasant

_____ c. awful

_____ Score 3 points for each correct C answer.

_____ Score 2 points for each correct O answer.

_____ **Total Score:** Using Words Precisely

Enter the four total scores in the spaces below, and add them together to find your Reading Comprehension Score. Then record your score on the graph on page 103.

Score	Question Type	Lesson 6
_____	Finding the Main Idea	
_____	Recalling Facts	
_____	Making Inferences	
_____	Using Words Precisely	
_____	**Reading Comprehension Score**	

Author's Approach

Put an X in the box next to the correct answer.

1. The authors use the first sentence of the article to
   - ☐ a. inform the reader about Sven Hedin.
   - ☐ b. get the reader's attention.
   - ☐ c. describe the Takla Makan desert.

2. What do the authors mean by the statement, "Still, the Swedish explorer felt a strong pull to investigate this Asian desert"?
   - ☐ a. Sven Hedin thought the Takla Makan desert was interesting.
   - ☐ b. Sven Hedin had a strong interest in exploring the Takla Makan desert.
   - ☐ c. Sven Hedin felt a mysterious force pulling him into the desert.

3. What is the authors' purpose in writing "Desert Disaster"?
   - ☐ a. to inform the reader about Hedin's expedition
   - ☐ b. to express an opinion about Hedin's expedition
   - ☐ c. to describe the qualities of the Takla Makan desert

---

_____ Number of correct answers

Record your personal assessment of your work on the Critical Thinking Chart on page 104.

Summarizing and Paraphrasing

Follow the directions provided for questions 1 and 2. Put an X in the box next to the correct answer for question 3.

1. Reread paragraph 8 in the article. Below, write a summary of the paragraph in no more than 25 words.

_____

_____

_____

_____

Reread your summary and decide whether it covers the important ideas in the paragraph. Next, decide how to shorten the summary to 15 words or less without leaving out any essential information. Write this summary below.

_____

_____

_____

_____

2. Read the statement from the article below. Then read the paraphrase of that statement. Choose the reason that best tells why the paraphrase does not say the same thing as the statement.

   Statement: "Grimly, Hedin cut everyone's water rations way down."

   Paraphrase: Hedin only allowed each person a cup of water per day.

   ☐ a. Paraphrase says too much.

   ☐ b. Paraphrase doesn't say enough.

   ☐ c. Paraphrase doesn't agree with the statement from the article.

3. Choose the sentence that correctly restates the following sentence from the article: "Knowing they couldn't properly water eight thirsty camels, they decided to leave two behind."

   ☐ a. They knew they didn't have enough water for eight camels, so they decided to leave two behind.

   ☐ b. Because they didn't have enough water to wet down eight camels, they had to leave two behind.

   ☐ c. The camels were so thirsty that Hedin decided to leave two behind to find water.

   _____ Number of correct answers

   Record your personal assessment of your work on the Critical Thinking Chart on page 104.

Critical Thinking

Put an X in the box next to the correct answer for questions 1, 2, and 5. Follow the directions provided for questions 3 and 4.

1. Which of the following statements from the article is an opinion rather than a fact?

   ☐ a. They said that evil spirits lurked in this vast stretch of sand.

   ☐ b. He had been into the desert before in search of gold.

   ☐ c. The next day Hedin discovered that they were almost out of water.

2. From what the article told you about the Takla Makan desert, you can conclude that

   ☐ a. no one has tried to cross it since Sven Hedin's expedition returned.

   ☐ b. many people died in the desert.

   ☐ c. the desert got very cold at night.

3. Which paragraphs provide evidence from the article to support your answer to question 2?

   _____

4. Choose from the letters below to correctly complete the following statement. Write the letters on the lines.

   According to paragraph 12, _____ because _____.

   a. no one had the strength to go back for him

   b. the group left Yollchi behind

   c. Islam Bai collapsed

5. Into which of the following theme categories would this story fit?

   ☐ a. important people in Chinese history

   ☐ b. desert dwellers

   ☐ c. desert crossings

   _____ Number of correct answers

   Record your personal assessment of your work on the Critical Thinking Chart on page 104.

Personal Response

I wonder why

_____

_____

_____

Self-Assessment

Before reading this article, I already knew

_____

_____

_____

A Jockey in Danger

People called it a freak fire. In 1983 a light bulb exploded in the jockeys' room at Oakland Park racetrack in Arkansas. The flames trapped Randy Romero, the only one in the room at the time. Other jockeys heard his desperate screams and pulled him to safety. But by that time the fire had burned nearly 60% of his skin.

2   Somehow Romero survived. But he had to spend months at a burn center. It was pure agony. Most nights he couldn't sleep. Sometimes the screams of other burn victims kept him awake. Other times he kept them awake with *his* screams. One of the most painful treatments involved being lowered

Jockey Randy Romero celebrates a win at Churchill Downs.

into a pool of warm water. The doctors then peeled off his dead, charred skin. After the skin was removed, new skin had to be grafted onto his body. "It was a nightmare," said Romero.

3   The doctors told Romero he was lucky to be alive. They said that he shouldn't think about riding horses again. But being a jockey was what Romero loved. So less than four months after the fire, he was back at the track. He had to wear a pressure suit to help hold his new skin in place. But that didn't keep him out of the saddle.

4   The fire wasn't Randy Romero's only close call. He narrowly escaped death at least 20 times. He is in a dangerous profession. Falling off a horse can kill or paralyze any rider. In addition, if they fall, jockeys face the danger of being trampled by trailing horses in a race. Time after time, Romero was thrown to the ground when his mount fell during a race. Yet he was always able to walk—or at least crawl—away from such accidents.

5   By 1990 Romero was one of the best jockeys in the country. He had recovered from his horrible burns. He

was winning hundreds of races each year. His mounts had won purses worth over 50 million dollars. Then trouble struck again. On October 27 Romero rode the filly Go For Wand in a 1 million-dollar race at Belmont Park in New York. Romero's horse battled a horse named Bayakoa for the lead. The two were head to head with less than $\frac{1}{16}$ of a mile to go. Suddenly, Go For Wand's right front leg snapped. The horse went down hard, tossing Romero to the dirt.

6   Sadly, Go For Wand had to be put to sleep. When a horse breaks a leg, there is usually no other choice. Romero was lucky, though. He wasn't trampled by the other horses in the race. He did feel some pain in his side, however, so he went to the hospital to be examined. After a quick check Romero was back at the track. He rode in another race later that day. For the next three days, though, his side continued to ache. So he went back to the hospital for a more complete checkup. Doctors discovered he had eight broken ribs and a cracked shoulder.

7   Romero recovered from this accident just as he had recovered from

his earlier ones. "Randy's the bionic man," says his wife. "He has had screws in his shoulder and ankles. He still has a steel plate on the right side of his face. You tell me a bone, and he's broken it."

8   On February 15, 1991, however, Romero came close to pushing his luck too far. He was riding at Gulfstream Park in Florida. Once again his mount fell. He was sent sprawling on the ground. This time he was really hurt. The medics rushed him to the first-aid room. A fellow jockey, Chris Antley, stopped by to see how his friend was doing. He saw Romero lying on a table, still and pale. "I thought he was dead," said Antley.

9   Romero wasn't dead, but his left elbow was badly shattered. The doctors in Florida tried to fix it. They put his arm in a cast and gave him exercises to do. Romero stayed in the cast for nine months. During that time he couldn't ride. His inactivity caused him to gain weight. Soon he weighed 140 pounds, well over his racing weight of 115 pounds. It took Romero another four

months to lose weight and get back into shape.

10   At last he thought he was ready to return to racing. But in the 1992 Kentucky Derby, he learned that his elbow was far from healed. As he rode that day, his elbow broke again. "It just fell apart," said Romero. This time he hadn't fallen. He hadn't banged it in any way. The joint just broke apart while he was riding.

11   Romero was in a panic. Never before had something like this happened. "I've broken my ankles, my femur, my jaw, my cheek, my collarbone, all my ribs, [and] my hip. I always healed like that," he said, snapping his fingers.

12   After seeing a new doctor, Romero thought he knew what had happened. The elbow had not been properly set, so a bone had shifted. Instead of bending at the joint, it was bending at the point of the break.

13   Now Romero had to undergo another operation. This one took five and a half hours, but it worked. Romero made another of his remarkable

recoveries. Soon he was back in the saddle doing what he loved most.

14   People later asked him why he didn't just quit. They asked why he continued to risk injury and even death. He had earned enough money to retire. "This is all I want to do," he answered. "Sure, I've had a lot of bad luck, but I've had a lot of good luck too. A lot of people are worse off than I am. I can still do the one thing I love most."

A Finding the Main Idea

One statement below expresses the main idea of the article. One statement is too general, or too broad. The other statement explains only part of the article; it is too narrow. Label the statements using the following key:

M—Main Idea　　**B—Too Broad**　　**N—Too Narrow**

_____ 1. Jockey Randy Romero has suffered over 20 serious accidents during his career, but each time he has been able to recover and return to racing.

_____ 2. Jockey Randy Romero has had many close calls during his career.

_____ 3. Nearly 60% of Randy Romero's skin was burned in a freak fire in 1983.

_____ Score 15 points for a correct M answer.

_____ Score 5 points for each correct B or N answer.

_____ **Total Score:** Finding the Main Idea

B Recalling Facts

How well do you remember the facts in the article? Put an X in the box next to the answer that correctly completes each statement about the article.

1. While Randy Romero was recovering in the burn center,
   - ☐ a. old skin was removed, and new skin was grafted onto his body.
   - ☐ b. he screamed every night.
   - ☐ c. he wore a pressure suit to keep his skin in place.

2. When Romero was riding the horse Go For Wand,
   - ☐ a. he won over $50 million.
   - ☐ b. the horse Bayakoa beat them by $\frac{1}{16}$ of a mile.
   - ☐ c. the horse's right front leg snapped.

3. It took Romero longest to recover from an injury to his
   - ☐ a. ribs.
   - ☐ b. elbow.
   - ☐ c. leg.

4. After the second operation on his elbow,
   - ☐ a. Romero's joint just fell apart.
   - ☐ b. Romero wore a cast for nine months.
   - ☐ c. Romero soon returned to riding.

5. According to Romero, he continues to ride even after his many injuries because he
   - ☐ a. loves being a jockey.
   - ☐ b. doesn't have enough money to retire.
   - ☐ c. can't do anything else.

Score 5 points for each correct answer.

_____ **Total Score:** Recalling Facts

C | Making Inferences

When you combine your own experience with information from a text to draw a conclusion that is not directly stated in that text, you are making an inference. Below are five statements that may or may not be inferences based on information in the article. Label the statements using the following key:

C—Correct Inference   F—Faulty Inference

_____ 1. Randy Romero is a determined person.

_____ 2. Most jockeys have had many broken bones.

_____ 3. It is common for horses to break their legs while racing.

_____ 4. Randy's wife would like him to stop riding horses.

_____ 5. Jockeys cannot weigh very much.

Score 5 points for each correct answer.

_____ **Total Score:** Making Inferences

D | Using Words Precisely

Each numbered sentence below contains an underlined word or phrase from the article. Following the sentence are three definitions. One definition is closest to the meaning of the underlined word. One definition is opposite or nearly opposite. Label those two definitions using the following key; do not label the remaining definition.

C—Closest   O—Opposite or Nearly Opposite

1. It was pure <u>agony</u>.

_____ a. great pain

_____ b. pleasure

_____ c. frustration

2. After the skin was removed, new skin had to be <u>grafted</u> onto his body.

_____ a. taken off

_____ b. stretched

_____ c. attached

3. At least 20 times he <u>narrowly</u> escaped death.

_____ a. almost

_____ b. barely

_____ c. easily

4. Romero wasn't dead, but his left elbow was <u>shattered</u>.

_____ a. broken

_____ b. healed

_____ c. cut

5. Romero made another of his <u>remarkable</u> recoveries.

_____ a. ordinary

_____ b. strange

_____ c. amazing

_____ Score 3 points for each correct C answer.

_____ Score 2 points for each correct O answer.

_____ **Total Score:** Using Words Precisely

Enter the four total scores in the spaces below, and add them together to find your Reading Comprehension Score. Then record your score on the graph on page 103.

Score	Question Type	Lesson 7
_____	Finding the Main Idea	
_____	Recalling Facts	
_____	Making Inferences	
_____	Using Words Precisely	
_____	**Reading Comprehension Score**	

Author's Approach

Put an X in the box next to the correct answer.

1. The main purpose of the first paragraph is to

☐ a. introduce Randy Romero.

☐ b. describe one of Romero's close calls.

☐ c. describe the fire at the Oakland Park racetrack.

2. Which of the following statements from the article best describes Randy Romero?

☐ a. "Randy's the bionic man," says his wife.

☐ b. Romero made another of his remarkable recoveries.

☐ c. But being a jockey was what Romero loved. So less than four months after the fire, he was back at the track.

3. The authors tell this story mainly by

☐ a. comparing different topics.

☐ b. telling different stories about the same topic.

☐ c. retelling their personal experiences.

_____ Number of correct answers

Record your personal assessment of your work on the Critical Thinking Chart on page 104.

Summarizing and Paraphrasing

Follow the directions provided for questions 1 and 2. Put an X in the box next to the correct answer for question 3.

1. Look for the important ideas and events in paragraphs 1 and 2. Summarize those paragraphs in one or two sentences.

_____

_____

_____

_____

2. Complete the following one-sentence summary of the article using the lettered phrases from the phrase bank below. Write the letters on the lines.

> **Phrase bank:**
> a. other injuries he has had
> b. a description of the fire that burned nearly 60% of his skin
> c. an explanation of why he continues riding

The article about Randy Romero begins with _____, goes on to tell about _____, and ends with _____.

3. Choose the best one-sentence paraphrase for the following sentence from the article: "Time after time, Romero was thrown to the ground when his mount fell during a race."

☐ a. Romero fell off his horse many times while racing.

☐ b. Many times Romero fell to the ground while mounting his horse during a race.

☐ c. Several times Romero's horse fell during a race, and he was thrown to the ground.

> _____ Number of correct answers
>
> Record your personal assessment of your work on the Critical Thinking Chart on page 104.

Critical Thinking

Follow the directions provided for questions 1, 4, and 5. Put an X in the box next to the correct answer for questions 3 and 4.

1. For each statement below, write *O* if it expresses an opinion or *F* if it expresses a fact.

_____ a. Sometimes the screams of other burn victims kept him awake.

_____ b. They said that he shouldn't think about riding horses again.

_____ c. Suddenly, Go For Wand's right front leg snapped.

2. From what the article told you about Randy Romero, you can predict that he

☐ a. is still riding horses.

☐ b. has not been injured since 1992.

☐ c. has retired.

3. What caused Romero's elbow to break a second time?

☐ a. His horse fell.

☐ b. It had not been properly set the first time.

☐ c. He had started riding too soon after breaking it the first time.

4. Which paragraphs provide evidence from the article to support your answer to question 3?

_____

5. Choose from the letters below to correctly complete the following statement. Write the letters on the lines.

   According to the article, _____ caused Randy Romero to

   _____, and the effect was that _____.

   a. Go For Wand's leg snapping

   b. he broke eight ribs and cracked his shoulder

   c. fall to the ground

   ┌───┐
   │ _____ Number of correct answers   │
   │   │
   │ Record your personal assessment of your work on the │
   │ Critical Thinking Chart on page 104.   │
   └───┘

Personal Response

What was most surprising or interesting to you about this article?

_____

_____

_____

_____

Self-Assessment

I can't really understand how

_____

_____

_____

_____

Escape to Freedom

This train, pulled by a steam locomotive, is the type that carried Frederick Douglass to freedom.

Frederick Douglass's mother died when he was just six years old. Douglass, who was a slave, ended up fending for himself. Every day he did the chores his masters required. At night he slept on the dirt floor of an old shack. He had no shoes, no coat, not even a decent pair of pants. He rarely got enough to eat. To fill his stomach, he sometimes took an egg from the barn or an ear of corn from the field. Other times he fought the dogs for crumbs from under the master's table.

2 In 1826, when he was eight years old, his Maryland owners sent him to the city of Baltimore. There he went to work for Hugh and Sophia Auld.

The Aulds treated him kindly. They gave him food, clothes, and a warm bed to sleep in. Sophia Auld even began teaching him to read, but her husband soon put a stop to that. Once slaves learned to read, he warned, they would start getting ideas out of books. Then they would become unhappy with their lives as slaves. They might even figure out a way to get free.

3   Douglass heard what Hugh Auld said. He decided to keep working on his reading, no matter what. As the years passed, Douglass found ways to improve his reading skills. He read old papers. He read posters and signs. At the age of 12, he paid 50 cents to buy his first book. One of the stories in the book was about a slave who read so well and knew so much that he was able to talk his master into setting him free. That story gave Douglass even more incentive to become a good reader.

4   By 1838 Hugh Auld had died, and Frederick Douglass had been sent to work in a Baltimore shipyard. It was there that he put together a bold plan. He decided to make a run for freedom. In order to succeed, he would have to get out of Maryland. He would have to make it to one of the northern states, where slavery was illegal. Douglass knew that if he were caught he would be whipped and chained. He might even be killed. But he was willing to risk death for the chance to be free.

5   Douglass already knew some blacks who were free. Known as "freemen," each of them carried "free papers." The documents proved that the holder was free and not a slave. Once in a while, a slave would borrow someone's "free papers" to make an escape. When the runaway reached a free state, he or she would send the papers back. The trick was to get the papers from someone who looked like you. The papers stated such things as height, weight, color of skin, any scars, and so forth.

6   Douglass did not know any freemen who looked much like him. He did, however, have a black friend who was a sailor. This man had a set of papers stating that he was a free American sailor. At the top of the page was an American eagle. It looked very impressive. Douglass thought that these papers might work like "free papers." Unfortunately, the papers called for someone with skin much darker than Douglass's. Still, Douglass decided it was worth a chance. He would use the sailor's papers to make a break for freedom.

7   From Maryland the nearest free state was Pennsylvania. The best way to get there was by train. But Douglass couldn't just walk into the train station and buy a ticket. His papers would be checked too closely. So he waited until the train was pulling out of the station. Only then did he hop on board. He

A young Frederick Douglass

was dressed in a borrowed sailor's suit. He tried to look calm, but every nerve inside his body was on edge.

8   After a while, the conductor began checking tickets. When he got to the car carrying blacks, he also checked their papers. The conductor acted rude to some of the people in the car. This made Douglass even more nervous. But the conductor's face brightened when he got to Douglass. Perhaps it was because of the sailor's uniform. Most Americans had kind feelings for sailors at this time.

9   Still, the conductor had a job to do, so he said to Douglass, "I suppose you have your free papers?"

10   "No, sir," answered Douglass. "I never carry my free papers to sea with me."

11   "But you have something to show that you are a freeman, haven't you?"

12   "Yes, sir," said Douglass, "I have a paper with the American eagle on it."

13   Douglass handed over his papers to the conductor. The man barely glanced at them. He took Douglass's ticket money and left. Douglass was thrilled, but he was not out of danger yet. He was still in Maryland. He might be discovered and arrested at any moment. "I saw on the train several persons who would have known me in any other clothes," wrote Douglass. Amazingly, the sailor's uniform seemed to fool them all.

14   Slowly, the train moved north. To Frederick Douglass the minutes seemed like hours. At one station Douglass looked out the window and caught his breath. Just a few feet away was a man named Captain McGowan. Douglass had done work for him earlier that week. If McGowan noticed him, Douglass's plan would be foiled. Luckily, McGowan didn't look Douglass's way.

15   "This was not my only hair-breadth escape," wrote Douglass. At one point a German blacksmith who knew Douglass well looked straight at him. After a few seconds, he went back about his business. "I really believe he knew me," wrote Douglass, "but had no heart to betray me."

16   At last Douglass reached Philadelphia, Pennsylvania. Quietly but joyfully, he moved on to New York City. In less than 24 hours, he had gone from being a slave to being a free man. "No man now had a right to call me his slave," wrote Douglass.

17   Douglass kept the details of his escape a secret for more than 40 years. He didn't want to hurt other slaves who might use the same plan. Escaping was hard enough without giving away any secrets to slave owners. Also, Douglass didn't want to cause trouble for anyone who had helped him. Helping a slave to escape was a high crime. As Douglass said, "Murder itself was not more sternly punished."

18   Frederick Douglass went on to become world famous. He spent years fighting slavery. He published his own newspaper, called *The North Star*. Douglass wrote best-selling books about his life. He made friends with white leaders such as Abraham Lincoln. He urged the president to free the slaves. In 1863 Lincoln freed all the slaves in the southern states. So Douglass, who died in 1895, lived to see his people freed.

19   Over the years Frederick Douglass was often asked how his first day of freedom felt. He said, "I felt as one might feel upon escape from a den of hungry lions." He added, "My chains were broken, and the victory brought me unspeakable joy."

If you have been timed while reading this article, enter your reading time below. Then turn to the Words-per-Minute Table on page 101 and look up your reading speed (words per minute). Enter your reading speed on the graph on page 102.

Reading Time: Lesson 8

_____ : _____
Minutes   Seconds

A | Finding the Main Idea

One statement below expresses the main idea of the article. One statement is too general, or too broad. The other statement explains only part of the article; it is too narrow. Label the statements using the following key:

M—Main Idea   B—Too Broad   N—Too Narrow

_____ 1. Frederick Douglass was a slave who escaped to the north and gained his freedom.

_____ 2. Frederick Douglass learned to read from Sophia Auld, one of his owners when he was a boy.

_____ 3. Frederick Douglass escaped from slavery on a dangerous journey north by train using borrowed papers from a friend who was a free American sailor.

_____ Score 15 points for a correct M answer.

_____ Score 5 points for each correct B or N answer.

_____ **Total Score:** Finding the Main Idea

B | Recalling Facts

How well do you remember the facts in the article? Put an X in the box next to the answer that correctly completes each statement about the article.

1. When Douglass was sent to work for the Aulds in Maryland,
   - ☐ a. he slept on the dirt floor of an old shack.
   - ☐ b. Sophia Auld began teaching him to read.
   - ☐ c. he worked in a shipyard.

2. While Douglass was working in a Baltimore shipyard, he
   - ☐ a. made a plan to escape to the North.
   - ☐ b. decided to run to Pennsylvania.
   - ☐ c. thought he might be killed.

3. Many slaves who wanted to be free
   - ☐ a. became sailors.
   - ☐ b. borrowed a free black person's "free papers."
   - ☐ c. took trains to the North.

4. When Douglass was on the train to Pennsylvania,
   - ☐ a. he wore a borrowed sailor's suit.
   - ☐ b. the train conductor was rude to him.
   - ☐ c. some people recognized him.

5. After Douglass gained his freedom, he
   - ☐ a. became a politician.
   - ☐ b. convinced Abraham Lincoln to free the slaves.
   - ☐ c. published several books and a newspaper.

Score 5 points for each correct answer.

_____ **Total Score:** Recalling Facts

C Making Inferences

When you combine your own experience with information from a text to draw a conclusion that is not directly stated in that text, you are making an inference. Below are five statements that may or may not be inferences based on information in the article. Label the statements using the following key:

C—Correct Inference   F—Faulty Inference

_____ 1. Frederick Douglass did not know who his father was.

_____ 2. Many free blacks helped slaves gain freedom.

_____ 3. Slaves often worked for several different owners during their lives.

_____ 4. It was illegal for slaves to ride trains.

_____ 5. In Douglass's time, blacks had to ride in separate cars on trains.

Score 5 points for each correct answer.

_____ **Total Score:** Making Inferences

D Using Words Precisely

Each numbered sentence below contains an underlined word or phrase from the article. Following the sentence are three definitions. One definition is closest to the meaning of the underlined word. One definition is opposite or nearly opposite. Label those two definitions using the following key; do not label the remaining definition.

C—Closest   O—Opposite or Nearly Opposite

1. Douglass, who was a slave, ended up <u>fending for</u> himself.

_____ a. fighting for

_____ b. caring for

_____ c. neglecting

2. That story gave Douglass even more <u>incentive</u> to become a good reader.

_____ a. discouragement

_____ b. practice

_____ c. reason

3. It was there that he put together a <u>bold</u> plan.

_____ a. brave

_____ b. cowardly

_____ c. surprising

4. But the conductor's face <u>brightened</u> when he got to Douglass.

_____ a. changed

_____ b. grew angry

_____ c. cheered up

5. If McGowan noticed him, Douglass's plan would be <u>foiled</u>.

_____ a. successful

_____ b. good

_____ c. ruined

_____ Score 3 points for each correct C answer.

_____ Score 2 points for each correct O answer.

_____ **Total Score:** Using Words Precisely

Enter the four total scores in the spaces below, and add them together to find your Reading Comprehension Score. Then record your score on the graph on page 103.

Score	Question Type	Lesson 8
_____	Finding the Main Idea	
_____	Recalling Facts	
_____	Making Inferences	
_____	Using Words Precisely	
_____	**Reading Comprehension Score**	

Author's Approach

Put an X in the box next to the correct answer.

1. The main purpose of the first paragraph is to

☐ a. describe the life of a slave.

☐ b. describe Frederick Douglass's background.

☐ c. express an opinion about slavery.

2. What do the authors imply by saying, "Other times he fought the dogs for crumbs from under the master's table"?

☐ a. Douglass was fed the same food as the dogs.

☐ b. Douglass's master treated him like a dog.

☐ c. Douglass was so desperate for food that the would eat the food that fell from his master's table.

3. The authors probably wrote this article in order to

☐ a. make people aware of the terrible conditions in which slaves lived.

☐ b. inform people about Frederick Douglass's brave escape.

☐ c. explain why slave owners didn't want their slaves to learn to read.

_____ Number of correct answers

Record your personal assessment of your work on the Critical Thinking Chart on page 104.

Summarizing and Paraphrasing

Follow the directions provided for question 1. Put an X in the box next to the correct answer for questions 2 and 3.

1. Look for the important ideas and events in paragraphs 7 and 8. Summarize those paragraphs in one or two sentences.

_____

_____

_____

2. Below are summaries of the article. Choose the summary that says all the most important things about the article but in the fewest words.

☐ a. Frederick Douglass was born a slave. One of his masters started to teach him to read. This gave him the idea that he could be free. One day he made a run for freedom. He escaped to the North and became world famous.

☐ b. Frederick Douglass was born a slave, but he learned to read, made a daring run for freedom, and became a world-famous writer and advocate for ending slavery.

☐ c. Frederick Douglass escaped to the North and became a famous writer. He lived to see Abraham Lincoln free the slaves in 1863.

3. Read the statement from the article below. Then read the paraphrase of that statement. Choose the reason that best tells why the paraphrase does not say the same thing as the statement.

Statement: "That story gave Douglass even more incentive to become a good reader."

Paraphrase: That story helped Douglass to become a good reader.

☐ a. Paraphrase says too much.

☐ b. Paraphrase doesn't say enough.

☐ c. Paraphrase doesn't agree with the statement from the article.

_____ Number of correct answers

Record your personal assessment of your work on the Critical Thinking Chart on page 104.

✓

Critical Thinking

Put an X in the box next to the correct answer for questions 1, 3, 4, and 5. Follow the directions provided for question 2.

1. Which of the following statements from the article is an opinion rather than a fact?

☐ a. To fill his stomach, he sometimes took an egg from the barn or an ear of corn from the field.

☐ b. But he was willing to risk death for the chance to be free.

☐ c. "I really believe he knew me," wrote Douglass, "but had no heart to betray me."

2. Choose from the letters below to correctly complete the following statement. Write the letters on the lines.

According to paragraph 2, _____ because _____.

a. Sophia Auld stopped teaching Douglass to read

b. Douglass heard what Hugh Auld said

c. her husband warned her that it might give Douglass ideas about being free

3. From what Douglass said, you can conclude that

☐ a. not many slaves knew how to read.

☐ b. most owners treated their slaves poorly.

☐ c. most slaves going north went to Pennsylvania.

4. What did you have to do to answer question 3?

☐ a. find a cause (why something happened)

☐ b. find a reason (why something is the way it is)

☐ c. draw a conclusion (a sensible statement based on the text and your experience)

5. Into which of the following theme categories would this story fit?

☐ a. slaves in America

☐ b. trains in the 1800s

☐ c. from slavery to freedom

_____ Number of correct answers

Record your personal assessment of your work on the Critical Thinking Chart on page 104.

Personal Response

I know the feeling

_____

_____

_____

_____

Self-Assessment

What concepts or ideas from the article were difficult to understand?

_____

_____

_____

_____

Which were easy to understand?

_____

_____

_____

_____

Trapped in the Himalayas

The majestic peaks of the Himalayan Mountains offer little shelter to people stranded on them. Amazingly, Captains Rosbert and Hammel survived for several weeks in these mountains after their plane crashed into a mountain peak.

Pilots called it the "hump." That was an innocent-sounding name, but the reality was fearful. During World War II some pilots said they would rather fight Japanese war planes than challenge the hump. The "hump" was the Himalayan Mountains. Pilots had to fly over these Asian mountains—the highest in the world—to bring food and supplies to their Chinese allies.

2   How dangerous was the hump? In the early 1940s, 850 people died trying to fly over these mountains. The single worst day came in 1944 when nine planes crashed. The planes were not shot down. They simply

crashed into the mountains. Planes in those days were not as good as they are today. The Douglas C-47s had to strain to get high enough to clear the peaks. Some pilots joked grimly that they could plot their course by the line of smoking wrecks.

3   On April 7, 1943, Captain C. Joseph Rosbert took off in thick fog from India to fly over the "hump." His co-pilot was Captain Charles "Ridge" Hammel. A Chinese radio operator named Li Wong was also on board. As the plane neared the peak, Hammel reached back and gave Wong a reassuring pat. "We're O.K. now," he said. "Another thousand feet and we'll be clear of the hump. Another hour and you'll be home."

4   But they never made that thousand feet. Clouds moved in, and ice formed on the windshield. Ice also built up on the wings. Soon six inches of ice were weighing the plane down. The plane started to drop slowly. Rosbert pressed one hand to the windshield, hoping to melt the ice. He cleared a peephole two inches wide. Suddenly the cloud lifted, and Rosbert saw a jagged peak straight ahead. "Look out!" he yelled. "There's a mountain."

5   Rosbert banked the plane sharply as he kept his eyes on the tiny peephole. The plane missed hitting the peak by inches. But it swerved right toward a neighboring mountain. There was a terrible scraping noise. The men felt themselves thrown forward. The engines raced with a violent roar. Then, just as suddenly, everything fell quiet.

6   It took Hammel and Rosbert a couple of seconds to realize that they were still alive.

7   "What happened?" asked Hammel.

8   "We hit a mountain," answered Rosbert. Indeed, the plane had crashed sideways along the face of a cliff. Rosbert was surprised that they had survived; by all rights, he thought, they should be dead.

9   Sadly, the crash did end the life of Li Wong. The collision had broken his neck. Meanwhile, Hammel's face and hands were dripping blood. His left ankle was badly sprained. Rosbert, too, had hurt his left ankle. At least one bone had snapped. If it was a miracle that they had survived the crash, it would take a second miracle for them to get off this 16,000-foot mountain.

10   Rosbert and Hammel talked about what to do. They thought their chances of being seen and rescued were slim. They had no warm clothing and only enough food for a few days. When the sky cleared, they could see the tree line below. It was about 5,000 feet down and at least five miles away. If they could get there, they might find a stream. Then they could follow the stream down and maybe find a village. They decided that as soon as they could, they would head down toward those trees.

11   At the moment, though, neither man could walk. Their ankles hurt too much. So they stayed in the shelter of the plane. They figured that in five days their ankles might be healed enough to begin walking. By the third day, however, they couldn't stand the wait. They decided to head down the mountainside.

12   Each step was agony. After 200 yards they realized that they would never reach the tree line by nightfall. Knowing that they wouldn't survive a night in the open, they turned back. They were lucky to get back to the plane before dark.

13 The next morning Rosbert and Hammel used bits of wood from the plane to make splints for their legs. They hoped that would ease the pain of walking. They also used the wood to fashion a couple of crude sleds. The sleds didn't work very well; they went too fast and were impossible to control. But the men discovered that they could slide on the seat of their pants, going 20 or 30 yards at a time. In this way they made their way slowly down the mountain.

14 As they neared the tree line they reached a very steep 500-foot slope. There was no way to get around it. They would have to go straight down and hope for the best. Hammel went first, disappearing in a cloud of snow. All Rosbert heard was a loud scream. Moments later, Hammel shouted out, "It's O.K., but it's rough. Come on down."

15 Hammel took a deep breath, shoved off with his good leg, and began sailing down the slope. "Finally, I hit solid earth with a crunching jolt," he later said. "As I lay there, afraid my back was broken, I heard the sound of rushing water." The men's spirits rose. They had found a river.

16 For three days they hobbled along, following the river. By now all their food was gone. They had to find help soon or they would die. When the riverbanks became too steep, they moved down into the river itself.

17 Then they came to a series of dangerous waterfalls. They couldn't walk in the water any longer, but on both sides of them rose sheer walls of rock. How could they ever get out? Their situation appeared hopeless.

18 Then Hammel leaned forward. He had spotted a vine hanging off one of the cliffs. After pulling on it, he and Rosbert decided it might be sturdy enough to hold them. Besides, it was their only chance. "Foot by foot," said Rosbert, "we pulled and clambered our way up the wall." At the top they found an encouraging sign of human life. Someone had notched the trees as though marking a trail.

19 For the next several days the two men dragged themselves along, still following the river. Thirteen days after the crash, they came to a fork in the river. They weren't sure which way to go but at last decided to head east, the same direction they had been traveling all along. It was a lucky choice. Within an hour the men had stumbled upon a hut. It was burned to the ground, but at least it showed that people had once lived here. With renewed strength Hammel and Rosbert kept walking. Just before night they came to another hut. This one, thankfully, had people inside. The people looked like they had stepped out of the Stone Age. They had broad, flat foreheads and mops of long, shaggy hair. They were very hospitable and interested in their visitors. They gave Hammel and Rosbert food and a place to sleep. In return, the men let their hosts feel their clothes and look at their watches and flashlights.

20 For the next several days they stayed in the remote village. Although the people treated them very well, the men were still eager to get home. The natives helped them hike 16 more days to get out of the mountains. Finally, 47 days after the crash, they made it back to their base in India. No one could believe that they had survived such an ordeal. It was, as one magazine put it, "one chance in a million."

If you have been timed while reading this article, enter your reading time below. Then turn to the Words-per-Minute Table on page 101 and look up your reading speed (words per minute). Enter your reading speed on the graph on page 102.

Reading Time: Lesson 9

_____ : _____
Minutes   Seconds

A Finding the Main Idea

One statement below expresses the main idea of the article. One statement is too general, or too broad. The other statement explains only part of the article; it is too narrow. Label the statements using the following key:

M—Main Idea   B—Too Broad   N—Too Narrow

_____ 1. Pilots Rosbert and Hammel both hurt their legs when they crashed in the Himalayas.

_____ 2. After surviving a plane crash in the Himalayas, pilots Rosbert and Hammel struggled through the mountains for 13 days before being taken in by natives in a remote village who eventually helped them return to their base.

_____ 3. Pilots Hammel and Rosbert were lucky to survive a plane crash in the Himalayan mountains.

_____ Score 15 points for a correct M answer.

_____ Score 5 points for each correct B or N answer.

_____ **Total Score:** Finding the Main Idea

B Recalling Facts

How well do you remember the facts in the article? Put an X in the box next to the answer that correctly completes each statement about the article.

1. While flying over the Himalayan mountains during World War II, many pilots
   - ☐ a. were shot down by the Japanese.
   - ☐ b. crashed into the mountains.
   - ☐ c. saw native people living in the mountains.

2. Rosbert and Hammel were surprised that
   - ☐ a. radio operator Li Wong died in the crash.
   - ☐ b. ice formed on the windshield of the plane.
   - ☐ c. they survived the crash.

3. Rosbert and Hammel decided to head down the mountain because they
   - ☐ a. thought their chances of being seen and rescued from the top were slim.
   - ☐ b. thought it would lead them back to their base.
   - ☐ c. were not far from the bottom of the mountain.

4. To ease the pain of walking on their injured legs, Rosbert and Hammel
   - ☐ a. went down the mountain on sleds.
   - ☐ b. walked with canes.
   - ☐ c. made wooden splints for their legs.

5. Rosbert and Hammel made it back to their base in India
   - ☐ a. after hiking through the mountains for 16 days.
   - ☐ b. 47 days after the crash.
   - ☐ c. after 16 days of living with natives of the mountains.

Score 5 points for each correct answer.

_____ **Total Score:** Recalling Facts

C | Making Inferences

When you combine your own experience with information from a text to draw a conclusion that is not directly stated in that text, you are making an inference. Below are five statements that may or may not be inferences based on information in the article. Label the statements using the following key:

C—Correct Inference   F—Faulty Inference

_____ 1. Flying over the Himalayan Mountains was the only way for the Americans to get supplies to the Chinese.

_____ 2. During World War II planes did not have windshield defrosters.

_____ 3. Rosbert and Hammel's injured legs healed as they hiked down the mountain.

_____ 4. The native people Rosbert and Hammel met had never met Westerners before.

_____ 5. Rosbert and Hammel were the only people to survive a crash in the Himalayas during World War II.

Score 5 points for each correct answer.

_____ **Total Score:** Making Inferences

D | Using Words Precisely

Each numbered sentence below contains an underlined word or phrase from the article. Following the sentence are three definitions. One definition is closest to the meaning of the underlined word. One definition is opposite or nearly opposite. Label those two definitions using the following key; do not label the remaining definition.

C—Closest   O—Opposite or Nearly Opposite

1. Pilots had to fly over these Asian mountains . . . to bring food and supplies to their Chinese <u>allies</u>.

_____ a. armies

_____ b. enemies

_____ c. partners

2. The Douglas C-47s had to <u>strain</u> to get high enough to clear the peaks.

_____ a. struggle

_____ b. coast

_____ c. race

3. Rosbert <u>banked</u> the plane sharply as he kept his eyes on the tiny peephole.

_____ a. straightened

_____ b. reversed

_____ c. turned

4. They also used the wood to fashion a couple of <u>crude</u> sleds.

_____ a. fast

_____ b. simple

_____ c. well-made

5. They were very <u>hospitable</u> and interested in their visitors.

_____ a. friendly

_____ b. curious

_____ c. cold

_____ Score 3 points for each correct C answer.

_____ Score 2 points for each correct O answer.

_____ **Total Score:** Using Words Precisely

Enter the four total scores in the spaces below, and add them together to find your Reading Comprehension Score. Then record your score on the graph on page 103.

Score	Question Type	Lesson 9
_____	Finding the Main Idea	
_____	Recalling Facts	
_____	Making Inferences	
_____	Using Words Precisely	
_____	**Reading Comprehension Score**	

Author's Approach

Put an X in the box next to the correct answer.

1. The authors use the first sentence of the article to

☐ a. get the reader's attention.

☐ b. describe the "hump."

☐ c. describe how Americans brought food to their Chinese allies during World War II.

2. What is the authors' purpose in writing "Trapped in the Himalayas"?

☐ a. to describe the dangers of flying over the Himalayas

☐ b. to inform the reader about the primitive people living in the Himalayas

☐ c. to describe Rosbert and Hammel's amazing ordeal

3. The authors tell this story mainly by

☐ a. using their imagination and creativity.

☐ b. retelling the pilots' experiences.

☐ c. comparing different stories about the Himalayas.

_____ Number of correct answers

Record your personal assessment of your work on the Critical Thinking Chart on page 104.

Summarizing and Paraphrasing

Follow the directions provided for question 1. Put an X in the box next to the correct answer for questions 2 and 3.

1. Reread paragraph 13 in the article. Below, write a summary of the paragraph in no more than 25 words.

_____

_____

_____

Reread your summary and decide whether it covers the important ideas in the paragraph. Next, decide how to shorten the summary to 15 words or less without leaving out any essential information. Write this summary below.

_____

_____

_____

2. Read the statement from the article below. Then read the paraphrase of that statement. Choose the reason that best tells why the paraphrase does not say the same thing as the statement.

   Statement: "Someone had notched the trees as though marking a trail."

   Paraphrase: Someone had marked a trail through the trees.

   ☐ a.   Paraphrase says too much.

   ☐ b.   Paraphrase doesn't say enough.

   ☐ c.   Paraphrase doesn't agree with the statement from the article.

3. Choose the sentence that correctly restates the following sentence from the article: "Within an hour, the men had stumbled upon a hut."

   ☐ a.   Within an hour, the men had found a hut.

   ☐ b.   Within an hour, the men had been invited into a hut.

   ☐ c.   Within an hour, the men had gone into a hut.

_____ Number of correct answers

Record your personal assessment of your work on the Critical Thinking Chart on page 104.

Critical Thinking

Follow the directions provided for questions 1, 3, and 4. Put an X in the box next to the correct answer for questions 2 and 5.

1. For each statement below, write O if it expresses an opinion or F if it expresses a fact.

   _____ a.   Rosbert was surprised that they had survived; by all rights, he thought, they should be dead.

   _____ b.   They figured that in five days their ankles might be healed enough to begin walking.

   _____ c.   They had broad, flat foreheads and mops of long, shaggy hair.

2. From the information in the article, you can conclude that

   ☐ a.   most of the pilots who crashed into the Himalayas died.

   ☐ b.   Rosbert and Hammel were not worried about crashing as they flew over the hump.

   ☐ c.   The native people they met moved out of the mountains after meeting Rosbert and Hammel.

3. Choose from the letters below to correctly complete the following statement. Write the letters on the lines.

   On the positive side, _____, but on the negative side _____.

   a. they were rescued by natives of the mountains

   b. they were stranded at the top of the Himalayan Mountains

   c. Rosbert and Hammel survived the crash

4. Choose from the letters below to correctly complete the following statement. Write the letters on the lines.

   According to paragraph 19, _____ because _____.

   a. Rosbert and Hammel came across people who lived in the Himalayan Mountains

   b. they gave them food and a place to sleep

   c. they had decided to head east at a fork in the river

5. What did you have to do to answer question 4?

   ☐ a. find a reason (why something is the way it is)

   ☐ b. find a purpose (why something is done)

   ☐ c. find a contrast (how things are different)

   _____ Number of correct answers

   Record your personal assessment of your work on the Critical Thinking Chart on page 104.

Personal Response

I wonder why

_____

_____

_____

_____

Self-Assessment

I can't really understand how

_____

_____

_____

_____

Bear Attack

Trouble was about to break out on Mount Lemmon. For years the 9,000-foot peak north of Tucson, Arizona, had been a popular spot for hiking and camping. In the summer of 1996, however, the mountain was not a safe place to be. Danger was lurking behind the trees and in the shadows. The danger could be summed up in just one word: bears. A recent drought had dried up much of the bears' food supply. Now these animals were look- ing for food near human sites. Before the summer was over, two girls would learn just how fearsome hungry bears could be.

In 1996 a drought dried up much of the food supply of the bears on Arizona's Mount Lemmon, causing problems with bear attacks at campsites on the mountain.

2   Jennifer Corrales was the first victim. On July 13 eight-year-old Corrales was camping out on Mount Lemmon. She had come with her Girl Scout group. They were staying at Whispering Pines campground. As night fell, the girls and their adult leaders made "s'mores." They piled chocolate bars and marshmallows on top of graham crackers. That made a gooey but delicious treat.

3   When Corrales finished eating, bits of marshmallow and chocolate clung to her face. She didn't bother to wash up. Instead, she just climbed into her bedroll. She fell asleep under the stars.

4   Sometime that night, Corrales woke up. A huge hulking shape loomed over her. It was a bear! The animal leaned over and sniffed Corrales's face. Terrified, Corrales screamed. The bear swiped at her face with its giant paw. Then it turned and left the campsite.

5   Corrales was taken to the hospital. The bear had ripped the tear duct in her eye. Its claws had cut her face. Still, she was lucky. The damage could have been much worse.

6   After the incident the Arizona Game and Fish Department made plans to trap the bear and move it to a different mountain. Officials said it had become too bold. The same bear had recently gone into a cabin in search of food. It had also been seen tearing into an outdoor refrigerator. Officials were sure it was the same bear. A scar on its back made it easy to spot.

7   But this was not the only bear on Mount Lemmon. There were others, and most of them were hungry too. Every day the bears scoured the woods searching for food. Some found trash left by careless campers. A few prowled around cabins where people lived. One woman who lived on the mountain felt sorry for the bears. She began leaving food for them on her back doorstep. She meant well, but she really just added to the problem. As the bears became used to taking people's food, they lost their fear of humans. That made them more dangerous than ever.

8   Meanwhile, 16-year-old Anna Knochel was getting ready to camp out on Mount Lemmon. Knochel was part of a 4-H group from Pima County. The group had plans to camp at Organization Ridge. This was a popular campground on the mountain. Knochel's group had 71 children and 11 adults. There were also 14 counselors, one of whom was Knochel.

9   On the night of July 24, Knochel was on the mountain. It was dark when she and the others went to bed. Knochel was alone in her tent, but she wasn't worried. There were plenty of people in tents right near hers.

10   Unlike Jennifer Corrales, Anna Knochel went to sleep with a clean face. Her tent contained no food of any kind. Yet at 5:15 the next morning, a huge black bear pushed its way into her tent. As Knochel awoke, the bear attacked.

11   The 340-pound bear pounced on top of Knochel. She screamed at the top of her voice, but the bear didn't back off. Instead, it began ripping at her face and arms with its sharp claws. It sank its teeth into her shoulder and the top of her head. It also took a deep bite out of her right thigh.

12   "I'm being attacked by a bear!" Knochel shouted as blood poured from her wounds.

13 Other campers heard her cries. They ran to her tent and began banging on the canvas, hoping to drive the bear away. It didn't work. They shouted and screamed, but still the animal continued to maul Knochel. Someone yelled at Knochel to play dead. But that didn't seem to help, either. The bear kept on attacking her.

14 At last one of the adult chaperones came running with a handgun. The chaperone fired a bullet into the ground, sure that such a loud noise would scare the creature off, but the bear hardly seemed to hear the blast.

15 Desperate, the chaperone took aim at the bear. This shot hit the animal and wounded it. Now, at last, the bear stopped its attack. It turned and fled into the woods.

16 The horrified campers rushed to get help for Knochel. A helicopter came and airlifted her to Tucson Medical Center. She was in bad shape. She needed surgery right away. Most of her right thigh and buttock were gone. She was covered with cuts and puncture wounds. She had also lost a lot of blood. "It was a devastating injury for her," one of the doctors later said. "This kind of severe bear attack was a life-threatening injury."

17 As doctors worked to save Knochel, sheriffs back on Mount Lemmon tracked down the bear. They followed the trail of blood it had left. It took them about an hour. Then two deputies spotted the bear and shot it to death.

18 Anna Knochel survived the attack, but her life would never be the same. She had to have several operations. Even then, she needed a brace to walk. Knochel also had to deal with what her father called "pretty vivid memories." He said, "She didn't lose consciousness during the attack or after the attack. Obviously, she has a lot to deal with in terms of the whole incident."

19 Still, Knochel tried to look on the bright side. "Her spirit has been an inspiration to her nurses, to her doctors, to her family," said her father. "You can't sugarcoat this kind of injury. But she's been amazing as far as how she's been dealing with this."

20 Later, Anna Knochel was asked if she would ever return to Mount Lemmon. She might, she said. But she wouldn't stay the night.

A | Finding the Main Idea

One statement below expresses the main idea of the article. One statement is too general, or too broad. The other statement explains only part of the article; it is too narrow. Label the statements using the following key:

M—Main Idea **B—Too Broad** **N—Too Narrow**

_____ 1. A drought in Arizona in 1996 caused bears on Mount Lemmon to look for food near human campsites, resulting in at least two bear attacks on campers on the mountain.

_____ 2. Because a drought had dried up much of their food supply, bears on Mount Lemmon had to look elsewhere for food.

_____ 3. Anna Knochel was attacked by a bear as she camped at the Organization Ridge campground on Mount Lemmon.

_____ Score 15 points for a correct M answer.

_____ Score 5 points for each correct B or N answer.

_____ **Total Score:** Finding the Main Idea

B | Recalling Facts

How well do you remember the facts in the article? Put an X in the box next to the answer that correctly completes each statement about the article.

1. When Jennifer Corrales went to bed at Whispering Pines campground,
   □ a. there was a bear standing above her.
   □ b. pieces of chocolate and marshmallow were stuck to her face.
   □ c. she slept in a tent by herself.

2. When the bear attacked Corrales, it
   □ a. sank its teeth into her shoulder.
   □ b. ripped the skin off her face.
   □ c. ripped a tear duct in her eye.

3. Because the bears on Mount Lemmon were hungry, they
   □ a. prowled around cabins where people lived.
   □ b. attacked many careless campers.
   □ c. left their trash in the woods.

4. Other campers tried to drive away the bear that attacked Knochel by
   □ a. playing dead.
   □ b. shooting a gun into the air.
   □ c. screaming and shouting.

5. After the attack, Knochel
   □ a. was rushed to a nearby hospital.
   □ b. lost most of her right leg.
   □ c. never returned to Mount Lemmon.

Score 5 points for each correct answer.

_____ **Total Score:** Recalling Facts

C Making Inferences

When you combine your own experience with information from a text to draw a conclusion that is not directly stated in that text, you are making an inference. Below are five statements that may or may not be inferences based on information in the article. Label the statements using the following key:

C—Correct Inference   F—Faulty Inference

_____ 1. Before 1996 the bears on Mount Lemmon did not usually bother campers.

_____ 2. Bears like sweets.

_____ 3. Most bears are afraid of humans.

_____ 4. Anna Knochel had never camped on Mount Lemmon before 1996.

_____ 5. Anna Knochel was not afraid of bears before 1996.

Score 5 points for each correct answer.

_____ **Total Score:** Making Inferences

D Using Words Precisely

Each numbered sentence below contains an underlined word or phrase from the article. Following the sentence are three definitions. One definition is closest to the meaning of the underlined word. One definition is opposite or nearly opposite. Label those two definitions using the following key; do not label the remaining definition.

C—Closest   O—Opposite or Nearly Opposite

1. A recent <u>drought</u> had dried up much of the bears' food supply.

_____ a. dry spell

_____ b. flood

_____ c. heat wave

2. When Corrales finished eating, bits of marshmallow and chocolate <u>clung to</u> her face.

_____ a. fell from

_____ b. covered

_____ c. stuck to

3. They shouted and screamed, but still the animal continued to <u>maul</u> Knochel.

_____ a. hit

_____ b. attack

_____ c. pet

4. She was covered with cuts and <u>puncture</u> wounds.

_____ a. skin-piercing

_____ b. bloody

_____ c. surface

5. "It was a <u>devastating</u> injury for her," one of the doctors later said.

_____ a. painful

_____ b. terrible

_____ c. harmless

_____ Score 3 points for each correct C answer.

_____ Score 2 points for each correct O answer.

_____ **Total Score:** Using Words Precisely

Enter the four total scores in the spaces below, and add them together to find your Reading Comprehension Score. Then record your score on the graph on page 103.

Score	Question Type	Lesson 10
_____	Finding the Main Idea	
_____	Recalling Facts	
_____	Making Inferences	
_____	Using Words Precisely	
_____	**Reading Comprehension Score**	

Author's Approach

Put an X in the box next to the correct answer.

1. The authors use the first sentence of the article to

☐ a. inform the reader about Mount Lemmon.

☐ b. entertain the reader.

☐ c. get the reader's attention.

2. What is the authors' purpose in writing "Bear Attack"?

☐ a. to emphasize how dangerous bears can be

☐ b. to inform the reader about the bear attacks on Mount Lemmon in 1996

☐ c. to persuade the reader not to camp on Mount Lemmon

3. The authors tell this story mainly by

☐ a. telling different stories about the same topic.

☐ b. using their imagination and creativity.

☐ c. comparing different topics.

_____ Number of correct answers

Record your personal assessment of your work on the Critical Thinking Chart on page 104.

Summarizing and Paraphrasing

Follow the directions provided for questions 1 and 2. Put an X in the box next to the correct answer for question 3.

1. Look for the important ideas and events in paragraphs 6 and 7. Summarize those paragraphs in one or two sentences.

_____

_____

_____

_____

2. Complete the following one-sentence summary of the article using the lettered phrases from the phrase bank below. Write the letters on the lines.

> **Phrase bank:**
> a. what happened to Jennifer Corrales
> b. an explanation of why bear attacks were a problem on Mount Lemmon in 1996
> c. a description of the attack on Anna Knochel

The article about bear attacks begins with _____, goes on

to explain _____, and ends with _____.

3. Choose the best one-sentence paraphrase for the following sentence from the article: "Every day the bears scoured the woods searching for food."

☐ a. Every day the bears searched for food.

☐ b. Every day the bears hunted through the woods looking for food.

☐ c. Every day the bears ate the food they found in the woods.

> _____ Number of correct answers
>
> Record your personal assessment of your work on the Critical Thinking Chart on page 104.

Critical Thinking

Put an X in the box next to the correct answer for questions 1 and 2. Follow the directions provided for questions 3, 4, and 5.

1. Which of the following statements from the article is an opinion rather than a fact?

☐ a. Now these animals were looking for food near human sites.

☐ b. She meant well, but she really just added to the problem.

☐ c. Someone yelled at Knochel to play dead.

2. From the information in the article, you might predict that

☐ a. Anna Knochel will never return to Mount Lemmon.

☐ b. people no longer camp on Mount Lemmon.

☐ c. many bears were moved from Mount Lemmon in 1996.

3. Using the information in the article about the bear attacks on Jennifer Corrales and Anna Knochel, list at least two ways in which the attacks were similar and two ways in which they were different.

Similarities

_____

_____

_____

Differences

_____

_____

_____

4. Which paragraphs provide evidence from the article to support your answers to question 3?

_____

_____

5. Choose from the letters below to correctly complete the following statement. Write the letters on the lines.

According to paragraph 7, _____ because _____.

a. bears became used to taking people's food

b. the bears were hungry

c. people left their trash or purposely left food out for the bears

_____

_____ Number of correct answers

Record your personal assessment of your work on the Critical Thinking Chart on page 104.

Personal Response

What new question do you have about this topic?

_____

_____

_____

Self-Assessment

From reading this article, I have learned

_____

_____

_____

Compare and Contrast

Think about the articles you have read in Unit Two. Pick three articles in which you thought people showed courage. Write the titles of the articles in the first column of the chart below. Use information you have learned from the articles to fill in the empty boxes in the chart.

Title	How did someone in this article show courage?	How would you describe the main character(s) in this article?	Suppose you were (one of) the main character(s) in this article. Would you have made the same decisions this person did? If not, what would you have done differently?

Which of these close calls would be most likely to happen to you? Why?

_____

_____

Words-per-Minute Table

Unit Two

Directions: If you were timed while reading an article, refer to the Reading Time you recorded in the box at the end of the article. Use this Words-per-Minute Table to determine your reading speed for that article. Then plot your reading speed on the graph on page 102.

Lesson / No. of Words	6 / 1073	7 / 965	8 / 1180	9 / 1258	10 / 1040	Seconds
1:30	715	643	787	839	693	90
1:40	644	579	708	755	624	100
1:50	585	526	644	686	567	110
2:00	537	483	590	629	520	120
2:10	495	445	545	581	480	130
2:20	460	414	506	539	446	140
2:30	429	386	472	503	416	150
2:40	402	362	443	472	390	160
2:50	379	341	416	444	367	170
3:00	358	322	393	419	347	180
3:10	339	305	373	397	328	190
3:20	322	290	354	377	312	200
3:30	307	276	337	359	297	210
3:40	293	263	322	343	284	220
3:50	280	252	308	328	271	230
4:00	268	241	295	315	260	240
4:10	258	232	283	302	250	250
4:20	248	223	272	290	240	260
4:30	238	214	262	280	231	270
4:40	230	207	253	270	223	280
4:50	222	200	244	260	215	290
5:00	215	193	236	252	208	300
5:10	208	187	228	243	201	310
5:20	201	181	221	236	195	320
5:30	195	175	215	229	189	330
5:40	189	170	208	222	184	340
5:50	184	165	202	216	178	350
6:00	179	161	197	210	173	360
6:10	174	156	191	204	169	370
6:20	169	152	186	199	164	380
6:30	165	148	182	194	160	390
6:40	161	145	177	189	156	400
6:50	157	141	173	184	152	410
7:00	153	138	169	180	149	420
7:10	150	135	165	176	145	430
7:20	146	132	161	172	142	440
7:30	143	129	157	168	139	450
7:40	140	126	154	164	136	460
7:50	137	123	151	161	133	470
8:00	134	121	148	157	130	480

Minutes and Seconds

Plotting Your Progress: Reading Speed

Unit Two

Directions: If you were timed while reading an article, write your words-per-minute rate for that article in the box under the number of the lesson. Then plot your reading speed on the graph by putting a small X on the line directly above the number of the lesson, across from the number of words per minute you read. As you mark your speed for each lesson, graph your progress by drawing a line to connect the X's.

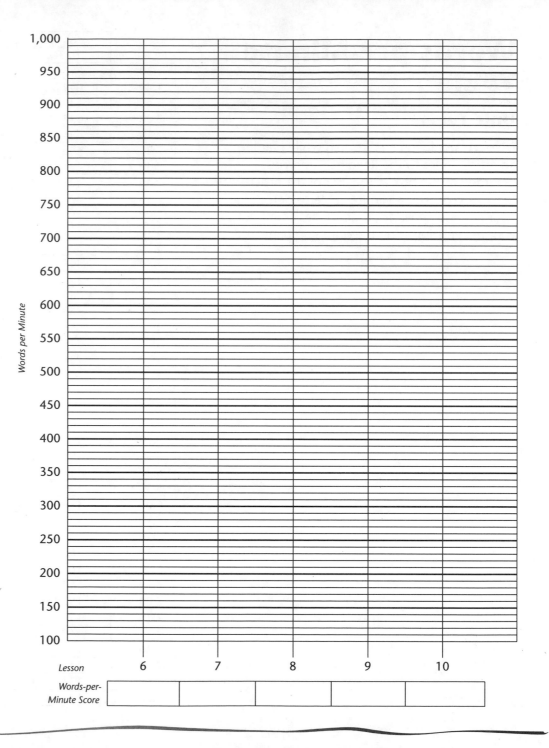

Lesson	6	7	8	9	10
Words-per-Minute Score					

Plotting Your Progress: Reading Comprehension

Unit Two

Directions: Write your Reading Comprehension score for each lesson in the box under the number of the lesson. Then plot your score on the graph by putting a small X on the line directly above the number of the lesson and across from the score you earned. As you mark your score for each lesson, graph your progress by drawing a line to connect the X's.

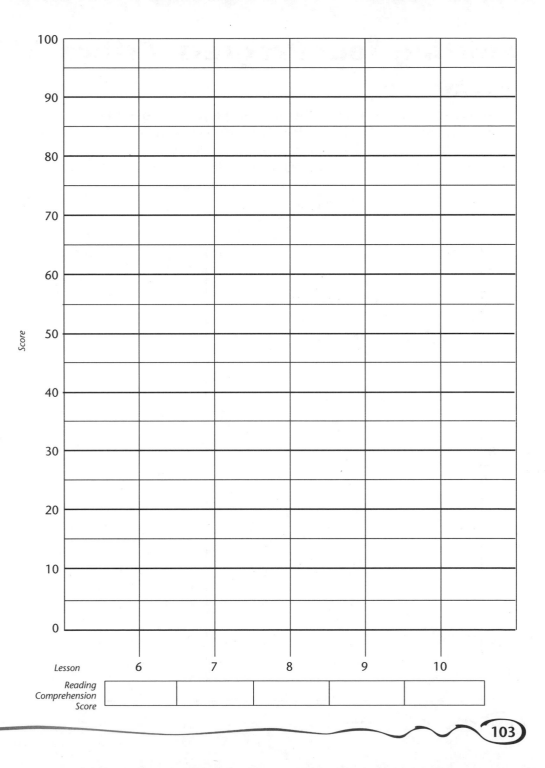

Score

Lesson	6	7	8	9	10
Reading Comprehension Score					

Plotting Your Progress: Critical Thinking

Unit Two

Directions: Work with your teacher to evaluate your responses to the Critical Thinking questions for each lesson. Then fill in the appropriate spaces in the chart below. For each lesson and each type of Critical Thinking question, do the following: Mark a minus sign (–) in the box to indicate areas in which you feel you could improve. Mark a plus sign (+) to indicate areas in which you feel you did well. Mark a minus-slash-plus sign (–/+) to indicate areas in which you had mixed success. Then write any comments you have about your performance, including ideas for improvement.

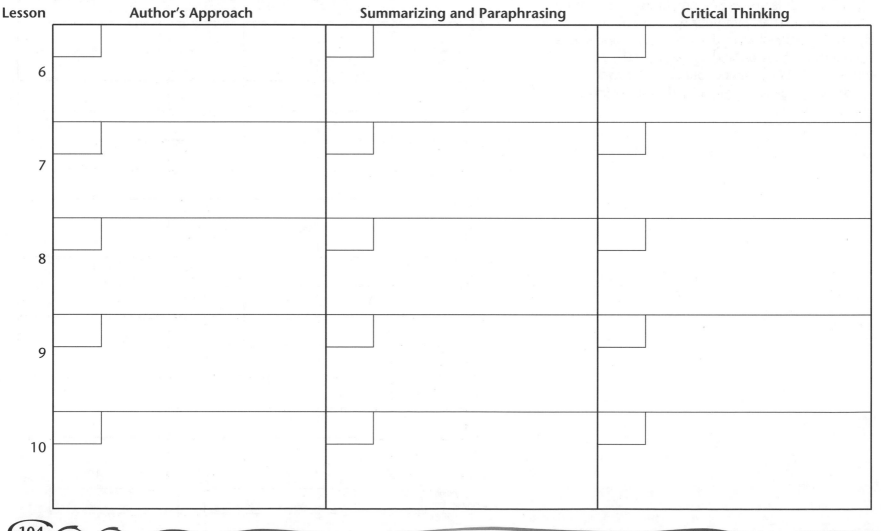

Lesson	Author's Approach	Summarizing and Paraphrasing	Critical Thinking
6			
7			
8			
9			
10			

UNIT THREE

All Alone in the Jungle

Juliane Koepcke was looking forward to

Christmas. The 17-year-old had just finished high school in Lima, Peru. Now she was headed back to her parents' house. She couldn't wait to get there. Mr. and Mrs. Koepcke lived deep in the Peruvian jungle. Although the Koepckes were German, they had spent years studying wildlife along the Amazon.

2   Mrs. Koepcke flew to Lima to help her daughter pack up. Then she and Juliane headed to the airport for the 90-minute flight to the jungle town of Pucallpa. It was Christmas Eve, 1971. Juliane had dressed up for the occasion. She wore a frilly white dress and her best high-heeled shoes. About midday she climbed into a Lockheed

The rivers of the Peruvian jungle wind through miles of uninhabited land.

Electra plane. Then she took her seat next to the window, three rows from the back. Her mother sat in the seat next to her.

3   The flight seemed to go smoothly. There was no hint of trouble as the plane approached Pucallpa. The passengers were told to put on their seat belts for landing. Then, without warning, the plane flew into a violent jungle storm.

4   "Suddenly we heard a loud noise," recalled Juliane later. "Looking out of the window I saw that the right wing was on fire."

5   Terrified, Juliane turned to her mother. Mrs. Koepcke looked at her daughter and said, "This is the end of everything." These were the last words Mrs. Koepcke would ever speak.

6   Juliane later said, "The next thing I knew, it felt like I was sitting in the air and then everything went black."

7   The plane had exploded in midair. Ninety-one of the 92 people on board died in the blast. Only Juliane Koepcke survived. She landed on the jungle floor, still strapped to her seat. Her only injuries were a broken collarbone and a cut on her upper

right arm. Experts say it is almost impossible to survive such a fall. Yet somehow Koepcke did it.

8   At first Juliane was in a daze. She lay in her seat and called out for help, but no one answered. All she heard was the screeching of jungle birds. Then she got out of her seat and looked around. She couldn't see well because her glasses had come off in the explosion. Still, she spotted some Christmas cakes lying on the ground and ate them hungrily. She looked around for her mother, but Juliane saw no sign of Mrs. Koepcke anywhere. In fact, she saw no sign of human life at all.

9   As darkness fell, it began to rain. Juliane crept under her airplane seat and huddled there throughout the night. The next morning she crawled out again. She knew that if she didn't find a way out of the jungle soon she would die, so she began walking. Before long she stumbled upon a row of three airplane seats lying face down. Hoping to find other survivors, Koepcke turned the seats over. Strapped to the seats were the dead bodies of three teenage girls, their faces covered with flies.

10   Feeling sick, Juliane moved on, struggling through thick bushes. Branches tore at her dress. Her shoes stuck in the soggy ground. Before long, she had lost one shoe completely. From time to time, she heard airplanes high overhead. She thought that they were probably looking for survivors from the crash. But they could not see her through the dense jungle foliage.

11   That night Juliane curled up under a tree. The next morning she began walking again. By this time her stomach was rumbling with hunger. She saw several things she thought might be edible, including fruit, mushrooms, even frogs. But her parents had warned her that many things found in the jungle were poisonous. She didn't dare take even a small bite of anything.

12   Over the next three days, Juliane covered many miles. She finally came to a river and began to follow it, thinking it would lead her to civilization. From time to time, she climbed into the water and swam along with the current, thinking that would be easier than walking. When she got out of the water, she felt leeches clinging to her body. Several times she passed crocodiles along the riverbank, but fortunately they didn't seem very interested in her.

13   Walking was no better. Her bare feet turned black and blue with bruises. The sun burned her back. Thorns cut into her skin, causing painful infections. Jungle flies burrowed into the open wounds and laid eggs. When the eggs hatched, Juliane could feel worms wiggling around underneath her skin.

14   On the fourth day Juliane spotted a lean-to near the edge of the river. Too tired to go any farther, she crawled inside it. The shelter didn't contain any food, but she did find some kerosene. She splashed some of it onto her cuts and, using a splinter of wood, tried to dig the worms out from under her skin.

15   For five days Koepcke huddled in the lean-to, growing weaker and weaker. At last, nine days after the crash, she heard voices. Looking out toward the river, she spotted three local hunters paddling by in a canoe. Struggling to the riverbank, Juliane managed to call out to them. At first the hunters were reluctant to approach her. Her gaunt face and bloodshot eyes frightened them. Also, they were not used to seeing girls with white skin and blond hair. They feared she might be some sort of demon.

16   Finally, though, they paddled over to the lean-to. Seeing Juliane's weak condition, they did what they could to help. One man offered her food while another poured gasoline over her body to draw out the worms under her skin. "I counted 35 worms that came out of my arms alone," Koepcke later said. Ten more came out of other parts of her body.

17   The men let Juliane rest overnight and then loaded her into their canoe and headed downriver. Seven and a half hours later they made it to a small outpost. At last Koepcke was safe. Plans were made to take her to her father. Rescue teams questioned her about the location of the downed plane. When searchers did finally find the remains of the plane, they were shocked. It had exploded into hundreds of bits and pieces. As one searcher said, "Only God knows how that girl survived."

If you have been timed while reading this article, enter your reading time below. Then turn to the Words-per-Minute Table on page 147 and look up your reading speed (words per minute). Enter your reading speed on the graph on page 148.

Reading Time: Lesson 11

_____ : _____
Minutes   *Seconds*

A Finding the Main Idea

One statement below expresses the main idea of the article. One statement is too general, or too broad. The other statement explains only part of the article; it is too narrow. Label the statements using the following key:

M—Main Idea   **B—Too Broad**   **N—Too Narrow**

_____ 1. Juliane Koepcke survived the plane explosion that killed her mother.

_____ 2. Juliane Koepcke survived a plane explosion that killed everyone else on board and spent nine days alone in the Peruvian jungle before finally being rescued by local hunters.

_____ 3. Jungle flies burrowed into Juliane Koepcke's skin and laid eggs while she made her way through the dense foliage.

_____ Score 15 points for a correct M answer.

_____ Score 5 points for each correct B or N answer.

_____ **Total Score:** Finding the Main Idea

B Recalling Facts

How well do you remember the facts in the article? Put an X in the box next to the answer that correctly completes each statement about the article.

1. As the Koepckes flew to Pucallpa,
   ☐ a. they flew through a severe storm.
   ☐ b. their plane exploded in midair.
   ☐ c. someone set the right wing on fire.

2. When Juliane Koepcke got out of her airplane seat in the jungle, she
   ☐ a. saw no signs of human life.
   ☐ b. looked for her glasses.
   ☐ c. immediately began walking, trying to find her way out of the jungle.

3. While she was walking through the jungle, Koepcke
   ☐ a. ate fruit and mushrooms that she found along the way.
   ☐ b. waved to the planes she heard overhead.
   ☐ c. did not eat anything.

4. When Koepcke called out to the hunters,
   ☐ a. they were frightened of her.
   ☐ b. they did not see her.
   ☐ c. she was frightened of them.

5. The hunters Koepcke saw
   ☐ a. put her in their boat immediately.
   ☐ b. took her to her father
   ☐ c. gave her food and helped her remove the worms from under her skin.

Score 5 points for each correct answer.

_____ **Total Score:** Recalling Facts

C | Making Inferences

When you combine your own experience with information from a text to draw a conclusion that is not directly stated in that text, you are making an inference. Below are five statements that may or may not be inferences based on information in the article. Label the statements using the following key:

C—Correct Inference   F—Faulty Inference

_____ 1. Juliane Koepcke knew her way around the jungle because her parents lived there.

_____ 2. The plane the Koepckes were flying in was hit by lightning.

_____ 3. Someone on the plane had been carrying Christmas cakes.

_____ 4. Koepcke did not speak Spanish.

_____ 5. Koepcke had had worms under her skin before.

Score 5 points for each correct answer.

_____ **Total Score:** Making Inferences

D | Using Words Precisely

Each numbered sentence below contains an underlined word or phrase from the article. Following the sentence are three definitions. One definition is closest to the meaning of the underlined word. One definition is opposite or nearly opposite. Label those two definitions using the following key; do not label the remaining definition.

C—Closest   O—Opposite or Nearly Opposite

1. But they could not see her through the <u>dense</u> jungle foliage.

_____ a. thick

_____ b. green

_____ c. thin

2. She saw several things she thought might be <u>edible</u>, including fruit, mushrooms, even frogs.

_____ a. delicious

_____ b. poisonous

_____ c. fit to eat

3. Jungle flies <u>burrowed into</u> the open wounds and laid eggs.

_____ a. came out of

_____ b. dug into

_____ c. sat on

4. At first the hunters were <u>reluctant</u> to approach her.

_____ a. unwilling

_____ b. afraid

_____ c. eager

5. Her <u>gaunt</u> face and bloodshot eyes frightened them.

_____ a. fat

_____ b. very thin

_____ c. pale

_____ Score 3 points for each correct C answer.

_____ Score 2 points for each correct O answer.

_____ **Total Score:** Using Words Precisely

Enter the four total scores in the spaces below, and add them together to find your Reading Comprehension Score. Then record your score on the graph on page 149.

Score	Question Type	Lesson 11
_____	Finding the Main Idea	
_____	Recalling Facts	
_____	Making Inferences	
_____	Using Words Precisely	
_____	**Reading Comprehension Score**	

Author's Approach

Put an X in the box next to the correct answer.

1. The main purpose of the first paragraph is to

☐ a. introduce Juliane Koepcke.

☐ b. entertain the reader.

☐ c. inform the reader about the Peruvian jungle.

2. What is the authors' purpose in writing "All Alone in the Jungle"?

☐ a. to describe the explosion of the plane in which the Koepckes were flying

☐ b. to express an opinion about Juliane Koepcke

☐ c. to inform the reader about Juliane Koepcke's amazing story

3. Which of the following statements from the article best describes the odds of Koepcke's surviving the plane explosion?

☐ a. Experts say that it is almost impossible to survive such a fall.

☐ b. [The plane] had exploded into hundreds of bits and pieces.

☐ c. "Only God knows how that girl survived."

_____ Number of correct answers

Record your personal assessment of your work on the Critical Thinking Chart on page 150.

Summarizing and Paraphrasing

Follow the directions provided for question 1. Put an X in the box next to the correct answer for questions 2 and 3.

1. Reread paragraph 9 in the article. Below, write a summary of the paragraph in no more than 25 words.

_____

_____

_____

_____

Reread your summary and decide whether it covers the important ideas in the paragraph. Next, decide how to shorten the summary to 15 words or less without leaving out any essential information. Write this summary below.

_____

_____

_____

_____

2. Below are summaries of the article. Choose the summary that says all the most important things about the article but in the fewest words.

☐ a. After the plane she was flying in exploded in midair, Juliane Koepcke survived nine days of hunger, leeches, and flies in the Peruvian jungle before finally being rescued by local hunters.

☐ b. After the plane she was flying in exploded in midair, 17-year-old Juliane Koepcke began walking through the Peruvian jungle trying to return to civilization. She did not eat anything during that time and was attacked by leeches and jungle flies before finally being rescued after nine days.

☐ c. It is amazing that Juliane Koepcke survived a midair airplane explosion and nine days in the Peruvian jungle.

3. Read the statement from the article below. Then read the paraphrase of that statement. Choose the reason that best tells why the paraphrase does not say the same thing as the statement.

Statement: "They feared she might be some sort of demon."

Paraphrase: They were afraid of demons.

☐ a. Paraphrase says too much.

☐ b. Paraphrase doesn't say enough.

☐ c. Paraphrase doesn't agree with the statement from the article.

_____ Number of correct answers

Record your personal assessment of your work on the Critical Thinking Chart on page 150.

Critical Thinking

Put an X in the box next to the correct answer for questions 1, 3, 4, and 5. Follow the directions provided for question 2.

1. Which of the following statements from the article is an opinion rather than a fact?

   ☐ a. There was no hint of trouble as the plane approached Pucallpa.

   ☐ b. Hoping to find other survivors, Koepcke turned the seats over.

   ☐ c. As one searcher said, "Only God knows how that girl survived."

2. Choose from the letters below to correctly complete the following statement. Write the letters on the lines.

   According to paragraph 11, _____ because _____.

   a. she saw several things she thought might be edible

   b. Koepcke didn't eat anything in the jungle

   c. she knew many things in the jungle were poisonous

3. Into which of the following theme categories would this story fit?

   ☐ a. survival in the jungle

   ☐ b. jungle ecology

   ☐ c. wildlife along the Amazon

4. From the events in the article, you can predict that

   ☐ a. Koepcke never flew in a plane again.

   ☐ b. Koepcke's father was surprised to see her.

   ☐ c. Koepcke and her father left Peru shortly after her return.

5. What did you have to do to answer question 4?

   ☐ a. find an opinion (what someone thinks about something)

   ☐ b. make a prediction (something that may happen in the future)

   ☐ c. find a reason (why something is the way it is)

_____ Number of correct answers

Record your personal assessment of your work on the Critical Thinking Chart on page 150.

Personal Response

How do you think Juliane Koepcke felt when she realized she was alone in the jungle?

_____

_____

_____

Self-Assessment

A word or phrase in the article that I do not understand is

_____

_____

_____

Hanging from a Cliff

John Muir, *pictured here with Teddy Roosevelt, was a skilled mountain climber and naturalist.*

S. Hall Young thought it would be fun to climb a mountain. He didn't have much experience, but how hard could it be? After all, he was only 29 years old and in fairly good shape. He did have problems with his shoulders—he had dislocated them 10 years earlier, and they were still weak—but he didn't think that would matter. He didn't plan on putting much weight on his upper body. Besides, he would be climbing with John Muir, the famous naturalist. Muir was known as a smart, strong climber. Young figured that if he had any trouble, Muir could help him out.

2   And so on a bright summer day in 1879 Young and Muir headed up an 8,000-foot peak in southern Alaska. "From the first, it was a hard climb," Young later wrote. After three hours, they passed the tree line. They began to scramble over rocks and boulders. Muir set a brutally fast pace. "It was only by exerting myself to the limit of my strength that I was able to keep near him," said Young. Yet Young did not complain. He knew that Muir was trying to get them to the top in time to see the sunset.

3   By late afternoon they were nearing the summit. However, the most difficult part of the climb still lay ahead of them. It was a wall of rock that seemed to shoot straight up. Young did not see how they could possibly get past it.

4   Muir, however, was undeterred. "We must climb cautiously here," was all he said. Then he began to scamper up the wall, finding tiny handholds and footholds as he went. Young followed as best he could, but he could feel his shoulders beginning to ache. "My strength began to fail," he later wrote, "my breath to come in gasps, my muscles to twitch."

5   At last Young came to the top of the wall. He was now only 50 feet from the peak, but he was exhausted, and he still hadn't caught up with Muir. Hurrying along, he came to a five-foot gap in the trail. Looking down, Young saw that the earth sloped away sharply for about 12 feet and then opened into a thousand-foot crevasse. Anyone who fell into that crevasse would tumble to his death.

6   Young figured that Muir had simply jumped across the gap. He thought he could do the same thing. But his exhaustion made him careless. As he prepared to jump, he stepped too close to the edge. Suddenly a rock gave way, and Young found himself falling down the 12-foot slope toward the crevasse.

7   Screaming, Young twisted his body around to face the slope. His arms struck the wall of the slope hard and instantly both shoulders became dislocated. "With my paralyzed arms flopping helplessly above my head, I slid swiftly down the narrow chasm," he later wrote. He dug his toes and chin into the gravel, trying desperately to halt his slide.

8   At last he came to a stop. His feet hung out over the crevasse and his arms lay useless above his head. Only by digging into the gravel with his chin was he able to hang on. "Every moment I seemed to be slipping inch by inch . . . " he remembered. "I had no hope of escape at all. The gravel was rattling past me and piling up against my head. The jar of a little rock and all would be over."

9   Suddenly, he heard John Muir's voice above him.

10   "My God!" cried Muir. Then, a few seconds later, Muir called, "Hold fast; I'm going to get you out of this."

11   Muir couldn't get to Young from the far side of the gap, and he couldn't jump back across because the edge had crumbled away, making the gap much wider. So Muir had to leave Young and circle around the mountain. It took him 10 minutes to get back to the top of the slope where Young had fallen.

12   By then, Young didn't think he could last another second. Cold wind whipped at his light clothing, and his shoulders throbbed with pain. It took all his energy to keep his muscles from

shaking. He was now hanging so far over the crevasse that any movement could send him to his death.

13   Carefully Muir lowered himself down the slope toward Young. At last he got close enough. He was standing on a narrow ledge. With one hand he held onto a small piece of rock that jutted out from the slope. With the other he grabbed the back of Young's shirt and waistband.

14   "Hold steady," he said. "I'll have to swing you out over the cliff."

15   With a powerful tug, he pulled Young out over the crevasse and held him dangling in midair. Then Muir swung Young toward him. As he did so he caught the collar of Young's shirt in his teeth.

16   "I've got to let go of you," Muir told Young through clenched teeth. "I need both hands now. Climb upward with your feet."

17   With that, Muir began pulling himself back up the steep slope.

18   "How he did it, I know not," Young later declared. "The miracle grows as I ponder it. The wall was almost perpendicular and smooth. My weight on his jaws dragged him outwards. And yet, holding me by his teeth as a panther her cub and clinging like a squirrel to a tree, he climbed with me straight up 10 or 12 feet, with only the help of my iron-shod feet scrambling on the rock."

19   When they got to the top of the slope, Muir set Young down on the ground. Young was wincing with pain from his dislocated shoulders. But he was grateful to be alive.

20   Muir managed to shove Young's right shoulder back into place. The left shoulder could not be moved, however, so Muir used a handkerchief to make a sling for Young's left arm. Then the two men began the long climb back down the mountain.

21   First, they had to get down the wall of rock that Young had barely been able to climb up. In the darkness Muir took Young on his back and carried him much of the way. Three times Young's right shoulder popped out of place again. Each time Muir yanked it back into position.

22   Around midnight they reached the bottom of the wall. They still had 10 miles to go to reach the base of the mountain. Hour after hour Muir pushed, pulled, and carried Young along. Young later said that Muir did "the work of three men, helping me along the slopes, easing me down the rocks, pulling me up cliffs, dashing water on me when I grew faint with the pain . . . . "

23   At last, at 7:30 the next morning, the two men reached the bottom. Wrote Young, "The shoulder was in a bad condition—swollen, bruised, very painful." It took five men four hours of pulling before they were able to wrench it back into place. But even during that painful procedure, Young knew he was a lucky man. He had come within a few inches of death, yet he had lived to tell about it.

If you have been timed while reading this article, enter your reading time below. Then turn to the Words-per-Minute Table on page 147 and look up your reading speed (words per minute). Enter your reading speed on the graph on page 148.

Reading Time: Lesson 12

_____ : _____
Minutes   Seconds

A | Finding the Main Idea

One statement below expresses the main idea of the article. One statement is too general, or too broad. The other statement explains only part of the article; it is too narrow. Label the statements using the following key:

M—Main Idea   **B—Too Broad**   **N—Too Narrow**

_____ 1. When S. Hall Young slid down a steep slope and dislocated his shoulders while mountain climbing, his friend John Muir had to make a daring rescue and help Young down the rest of the mountain.

_____ 2. S. Hall Young slipped down a steep slope while mountain climbing and had to hold on to the wall with his chin until he was finally rescued by his friend John Muir.

_____ 3. S. Hall Young and John Muir climbed an 8,000-foot peak in Alaska in 1879.

_____ Score 15 points for a correct M answer.

_____ Score 5 points for each correct B or N answer.

_____ **Total Score:** Finding the Main Idea

B | Recalling Facts

How well do you remember the facts in the article? Put an X in the box next to the answer that correctly completes each statement about the article.

1. John Muir climbed the mountain quickly because he
   - ☐ a. was a good climber.
   - ☐ b. wanted to reach the top by sunset.
   - ☐ c. wanted to challenge Young.

2. Young had difficulty climbing the wall of rock because he
   - ☐ a. had dislocated his shoulders years earlier, and they were still weak.
   - ☐ b. was not in good shape.
   - ☐ c. didn't have much experience in mountain climbing.

3. Young slid down the 12-foot slope because
   - ☐ a. his shoulders were weak.
   - ☐ b. he stepped too close to the edge and a rock slipped.
   - ☐ c. he could not jump far enough.

4. In order to reach Young, Muir had to
   - ☐ a. circle around the mountain.
   - ☐ b. jump back across the gap.
   - ☐ c. hang on to the wall with his chin.

5. As Muir and Young made their way down the mountain,
   - ☐ a. Young fainted from the pain of his dislocated shoulders.
   - ☐ b. Muir was able to shove Young's left shoulder back into place.
   - ☐ c. Muir pushed, pulled, and carried Young along.

Score 5 points for each correct answer.

_____ **Total Score:** Recalling Facts

C | Making Inferences

When you combine your own experience with information from a text to draw a conclusion that is not directly stated in that text, you are making an inference. Below are five statements that may or may not be inferences based on information in the article. Label the statements using the following key:

C—Correct Inference   F—Faulty Inference

_____ 1. Young hadn't told Muir that his shoulders were weak.

_____ 2. Muir had climbed the mountain that he and Young were climbing before.

_____ 3. Young did not know that he would have to climb walls of rock on the hike with Muir.

_____ 4. Muir was easily frightened.

_____ 5. There was no hospital near the base of the mountain that Young and Muir climbed.

Score 5 points for each correct answer.

_____ **Total Score:** Making Inferences

D | Using Words Precisely

Each numbered sentence below contains an underlined word or phrase from the article. Following the sentence are three definitions. One definition is closest to the meaning of the underlined word. One definition is opposite or nearly opposite. Label those two definitions using the following key; do not label the remaining definition.

C—Closest   O—Opposite or Nearly Opposite

1. "It was only by <u>exerting</u> myself to the limit of my strength that I was able to keep near him," said Young.

_____ a. relaxing

_____ b. running

_____ c. pushing

2. Muir, however, was <u>undeterred</u>.

_____ a. not afraid

_____ b. discouraged

_____ c. hopeful

3. "We must climb <u>cautiously</u> here," was all he said.

_____ a. slowly

_____ b. carefully

_____ c. recklessly

4. Young saw that the earth <u>sloped</u> away sharply for about 12 feet, then opened into a thousand-foot crevasse.

_____ a. straightened

_____ b. dropped

_____ c. slanted

5. "The miracle grows as I <u>ponder</u> it."

_____ a. think about

_____ b. feel

_____ c. ignore

_____ Score 3 points for each correct C answer.

_____ Score 2 points for each correct O answer.

_____ **Total Score:** Using Words Precisely

Enter the four total scores in the spaces below, and add them together to find your Reading Comprehension Score. Then record your score on the graph on page 149.

Score	Question Type	Lesson 12
_____	Finding the Main Idea	
_____	Recalling Facts	
_____	Making Inferences	
_____	Using Words Precisely	
_____	**Reading Comprehension Score**	

Author's Approach

Put an X in the box next to the correct answer.

1. The main purpose of the first paragraph is to

☐ a. give background information for the story.

☐ b. entertain the reader.

☐ c. describe S. Hall Young.

2. What do the authors imply by saying, "He didn't have much experience, but how hard could it be?"

☐ a. The climb would not be hard.

☐ b. Experience is not necessary to climb mountains.

☐ c. The climb would be hard.

3. The authors tell this story mainly by

☐ a. retelling Young's personal experiences.

☐ b. telling the story from different points of view.

☐ c. using their imaginations and creativity.

_____ Number of correct answers

Record your personal assessment of your work on the Critical Thinking Chart on page 150.

Summarizing and Paraphrasing

Follow the directions provided for questions 1 and 2. Put an X in the box next to the correct answer for question 3.

1. Look for the important ideas and events in paragraphs 3 and 4. Summarize those paragraphs in one or two sentences.

_____

_____

_____

_____

2. Reread paragraph 8 in the article. Below, write a summary of the paragraph in no more than 25 words.

_____

_____

_____

_____

Reread your summary and decide whether it covers the important ideas in the paragraph. Next, decide how to shorten the summary to 15 words or less without leaving out any essential information. Write this summary below.

_____

_____

_____

3. Choose the best one-sentence paraphrase for the following sentence from the article: "He was now hanging so far over the crevasse that any movement could send him to his death."

☐ a. He was leaning so far over the crevasse that he was afraid he would fall to his death.

☐ b. He was so far over the edge of the crevasse that if he moved at all he could fall to his death.

☐ c. He was so close to the edge of the crevasse that any movement could cause him to fall to the ground.

_____ Number of correct answers

Record your personal assessment of your work on the Critical Thinking Chart on page 150.

Critical Thinking

Follow the directions provided for questions 1, 2, 3, and 4. Put an X in the box next to the correct answer for question 5.

1. For each statement below, write *O* if it expresses an opinion or *F* if it expresses a fact.

_____ a. S. Hall Young thought it would be fun to climb a mountain.

_____ b. Young figured that Muir had simply jumped across the gap.

_____ c. Carefully Muir lowered himself down the slope toward Young.

2. Choose from the letters below to correctly complete the following statement. Write the letters on the lines.

On the positive side, _____, but on the negative side

_____.

a. Young dislocated his shoulders when he fell

b. Muir was a good mountain climber

c. Muir was able to save Young from falling into the crevasse

3. Which paragraphs provide evidence from the article to support your answer to question 2?

_____

4. Choose from the letters below to correctly complete the following statement. Write the letters on the lines.

According to paragraphs 7 and 8, _____ because

_____.

a. his shoulders had been dislocated

b. his feet hung out over the crevasse

c. Young couldn't grab onto the wall with his hands

5. What did you have to do to answer question 4?

☐ a. draw a conclusion (a sensible statement based on the text and your experience)

☐ b. find a purpose (why something is done)

☐ c. find a contrast (how things are different)

_____ Number of correct answers

Record your personal assessment of your work on the Critical Thinking Chart on page 150.

Personal Response

I know how S. Hall Young felt because

_____

_____

_____

Self-Assessment

I can't really understand how

_____

_____

_____

Buried in Nairobi

Boom! No one knew what the strange sound was. The workers at the Ufundi Cooperative House in Nairobi, Kenya, all heard it, but no one could identify the source. Had the noise come from nearby construction work? Had it come from a gun? Or had it been a grenade blast? Looking for an answer, many people in the building rushed toward the windows. It was about 10:30 in the morning on Friday, August 7, 1998.

2   Gaitara Ng'ang'a [pronounced enyah-ENYAH] was as curious as everyone else. The 48-year-old scrap-metal dealer did not work in the Ufundi House. He had just dropped by to see a friend. Still, he was curious

The Ufundi Cooperative House in Nairobi, Kenya, was completely destroyed in a bomb attack meant for the American Embassy building next to it.

about the noise he had heard and joined the crowd of people scurrying to the windows. Ng'ang'a tried to see out, but he couldn't get close enough to the glass. At least a dozen people had beaten him there.

3 Then, just 10 seconds after the first boom, there was a second blast. This one was truly massive. Some unknown terrorist had planted a huge bomb outside the building. The explosion was so powerful that it blew out windows a mile and a half away. People on the other side of town felt their buildings shudder. Nearby cars, trucks, and even a town bus caught fire.

4 It turned out that the real target of the terrorists was not the four-story Ufundi House. It was the American Embassy across the parking lot. But while the bomb did do great damage to the American Embassy, it totally flattened the smaller Ufundi House. In all, the blast killed 213 people. That made it one of the bloodiest terrorist acts ever. (The first blast turned out to be a grenade. Some people think it was used to draw workers to the windows in order to kill as many as possible with the bomb.)

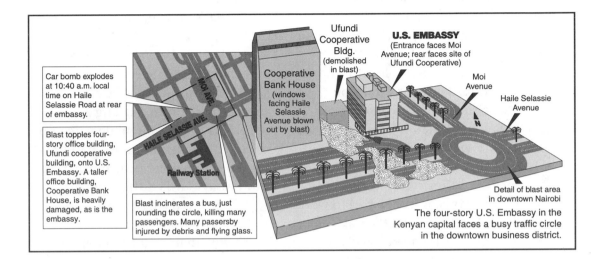

Car bomb explodes at 10:40 a.m. local time on Haile Selassie Road at rear of embassy.

Blast topples four-story office building, Ufundi cooperative building, onto U.S. Embassy. A taller office building, Cooperative Bank House, is heavily damaged, as is the embassy.

Blast incinerates a bus, just rounding the circle, killing many passengers. Many passersby injured by debris and flying glass.

Ufundi Cooperative Bldg. (demolished in blast)

Cooperative Bank House (windows facing Haile Selassie Avenue blown out by blast)

U.S. EMBASSY (Entrance faces Moi Avenue; rear faces site of Ufundi Cooperative)

Moi Avenue

Haile Selassie Avenue

Detail of blast area in downtown Nairobi

The four-story U.S. Embassy in the Kenyan capital faces a busy traffic circle in the downtown business district.

5 In all, the blast injured almost 5,000 people, As grim as this toll was, though, it could have been even worse. Thanks to a group of brave rescue workers, some people buried in the rubble were saved. One was Gaitara Ng'ang'a.

6 "I was lucky," he said. "I was not hit directly." The people who had rushed ahead of him to the windows took the full force of the blast and were killed. Ng'ang'a felt the building collapsing around him, burying him under a pile of concrete and steel. After the blast, he found himself trapped in a small clearing near some stairs. The space was just 4 feet high and 2 feet wide.

7 His left leg was broken and pinned under the rubble. Blood streaked down his face from deep cuts in his head, and some of his teeth were knocked out. Yet, incredibly, he stayed fairly calm. He recalled stories of people who had been trapped in collapsed buildings for days and were later saved. "I was expecting to wait two or three days," he said.

8 Ng'ang'a managed to reach into his pocket and pull out a match. Lighting it, he looked around. At the edge of the clearing where he sat there was a large hole. Even with a match, he couldn't see the bottom. He had no

idea how deep it was. He didn't want to find out the hard way. If the debris shifted, he might slip into the hole and fall so far that he would be killed. Ng'ang'a decided he had to get farther away from the hole, so he struggled to free his left leg. Using a cable wire that dangled overhead, he pulled himself up and away from the hole. Still, he was trapped under a mountain of debris. Sure that rescue workers were on the way, he fluffed up his coat into a pillow and went to sleep.

9   In fact, rescue workers had arrived on the scene. Soon they were sifting through the debris. But they had to work carefully. If they disrupted the balance of the rubble, the entire pile of steel and concrete could collapse. That would kill any survivors trapped underneath. "It is really a dicey operation trying to make sure nothing collapses on these people," said one of the rescuers.

10   Slowly, using tall cranes, they lifted slabs of concrete out of the way. They fired up blowtorches to cut steel rods. They used drills to slice through the smaller blocks of concrete. They also brought in specially trained dogs to locate some of the victims' bodies.

11   Meanwhile, rescuers kept calling out for anyone who was trapped. "Is anyone alive?" they shouted again and again. At last, the calls reached Ng'ang'a. By then he had been huddled in his little pitch-black space overnight. He had lost all sense of time. But he stirred himself and shouted out a response.

12   "Yes! Yes! Yes!" he yelled.

13   "What's your name?"

14   "Ng'ang'a!"

15   He kept hollering out his name. His calls helped rescuers determine exactly where he was. As they began digging down toward him, Ng'ang'a was surprised to hear a female voice not far away. It belonged to a woman who was buried somewhere near him. "What did he say?" asked the woman

16   "They are trying to save us," Ng'ang'a answered.

17   The woman said her name was Rose. Unlike Ng'ang'a, she was panicky. Her face was badly burned and she felt very thirsty. She desperately wanted to get out as fast as possible. She even asked Ng'ang'a if she could be rescued first.

18   But he had no control over that. Although Rose was near him, she was trapped in a place that was much more difficult to reach. As rescuers dug closer to Ng'ang'a, he tried to reassure Rose. "If I go," he said, "they will come next for you."

19   Then, at last, the rescuers broke through to Ng'ang'a. They could not pull him out right away. It took more hours of drilling and digging to free him. But at last, 36 hours after the blast, they lifted him out of the rubble.

20   The rescuers then went after Rose. They tried frantically to reach her in time. "I just told her to hold on, we're coming for her," said Bob Nasser, a Kenyan rescue worker. For a while, Rose answered him. "Yes," she kept saying. But rescuers could tell from her voice that she was very weak.

21   The last time anyone heard Rose speak was at 3 P.M. on Sunday afternoon. "Since then, we've heard nothing," said a Red Cross worker. "There's just no sound coming back."

22   Sadly, Rose did not survive long enough to be rescued. For Gaitara Ng'ang'a, the Nairobi bombing had been a close call. But for Rose and 212 other victims, it brought untimely death.

If you have been timed while reading this article, enter your reading time below. Then turn to the Words-per-Minute Table on page 147 and look up your reading speed (words per minute). Enter your reading speed on the graph on page 148.

Reading Time: Lesson 13

_____ : _____

Minutes   Seconds

A Finding the Main Idea

One statement below expresses the main idea of the article. One statement is too general, or too broad. The other statement explains only part of the article; it is too narrow. Label the statements using the following key:

M—Main Idea   **B—Too Broad**   **N—Too Narrow**

_____ 1. When a bomb was set off near the American Embassy in Nairobi, many people were killed.

_____ 2. When a bomb went off near the American Embassy in Nairobi, Gaitara Ng'ang'a found himself trapped in a small clearing near some stairs.

_____ 3. Gaitara Ng'ang'a was one of the few people lucky enough to be rescued from the rubble when a bomb destroyed the Ufundi Cooperative House in Nairobi.

_____ Score 15 points for a correct M answer.

_____ Score 5 points for each correct B or N answer.

_____ **Total Score:** Finding the Main Idea

B Recalling Facts

How well do you remember the facts in the article? Put an X in the box next to the answer that correctly completes each statement about the article.

1. Gaitara Ng'ang'a went to the window of the Ufundi Cooperative House
   - ☐ a. to see a friend.
   - ☐ b. because he saw other people going toward the windows.
   - ☐ c. because he was curious about a noise he had heard.

2. The bomb that went off
   - ☐ a. killed 213 people.
   - ☐ b. flattened the American Embassy.
   - ☐ c. was set by a terrorist group from Nairobi.

3. After the blast Ng'ang'a
   - ☐ a. called out to the rescuers.
   - ☐ b. remained calm and was confident that he would be saved.
   - ☐ c. panicked when he realized that he was trapped.

4. When Ng'ang'a called out his name to the rescuers,
   - ☐ a. a woman named Rose started calling out to him.
   - ☐ b. they did not hear him.
   - ☐ c. they were trying to rescue a woman named Rose.

5. Rescuers trying to reach Rose
   - ☐ a. could not hear her voice.
   - ☐ b. did not reach her in time.
   - ☐ c. did not know where she was.

Score 5 points for each correct answer.

_____ **Total Score:** Recalling Facts

C **Making Inferences**

When you combine your own experience with information from a text to draw a conclusion that is not directly stated in that text, you are making an inference. Below are five statements that may or may not be inferences based on information in the article. Label the statements using the following key:

C—Correct Inference   **F—Faulty Inference**

_____ 1. No one knew who set the bomb that flattened the Ufundi Cooperative House.

_____ 2. The Ufundi Cooperative House was part of the American Embassy.

_____ 3. The people who set the bomb did not like the United States.

_____ 4. Gaitara Ng'ang'a was the first person rescued.

_____ 5. Most of the people trapped under the rubble were rescued.

Score 5 points for each correct answer.

_____ **Total Score:** Making Inferences

D **Using Words Precisely**

Each numbered sentence below contains an underlined word or phrase from the article. Following the sentence are three definitions. One definition is closest to the meaning of the underlined word. One definition is opposite or nearly opposite. Label those two definitions using the following key; do not label the remaining definition.

C—Closest   **O—Opposite or Nearly Opposite**

1. Still, he was curious about the noise he had heard and joined the crowd of people <u>scurrying</u> to the windows.

_____ a. strolling

_____ b. pushing

_____ c. rushing

2. This one was truly <u>massive</u>.

_____ a. loud

_____ b. huge

_____ c. tiny

3. People on the other side of town felt their buildings <u>shudder</u>.

_____ a. shake

_____ b. stand still

_____ c. fall

4. Ng'ang'a felt the building <u>collapsing</u> around him, burying him under a pile of concrete and steel.

_____ a. falling

_____ b. breaking

_____ c. rising

5. Unlike Ng'ang'a, she was <u>panicky</u>.

_____ a. hurt

_____ b. calm

_____ c. terrified

_____ Score 3 points for each correct C answer.

_____ Score 2 points for each correct O answer.

_____ **Total Score:** Using Words Precisely

Enter the four total scores in the spaces below, and add them together to find your Reading Comprehension Score. Then record your score on the graph on page 149.

Score	Question Type	Lesson 13
_____	Finding the Main Idea	
_____	Recalling Facts	
_____	Making Inferences	
_____	Using Words Precisely	
_____	**Reading Comprehension Score**	

Author's Approach

Put an X in the box next to the correct answer.

1. The authors use the first sentence of the article to
   - ☐ a. get the reader's attention.
   - ☐ b. entertain the reader.
   - ☐ c. describe the bomb that exploded.

2. What is the authors' purpose in writing "Buried in Nairobi"?
   - ☐ a. to express an opinion about the bombing
   - ☐ b. to inform the reader about the bombing
   - ☐ c. to describe Gaitara Ng'ang'a's experience during the bombing

3. The authors tell this story mainly by
   - ☐ a. retelling one person's personal experiences.
   - ☐ b. comparing different views of the same experience.
   - ☐ c. telling different stories about the same topic.

_____ Number of correct answers

Record your personal assessment of your work on the Critical Thinking Chart on page 150.

Summarizing and Paraphrasing

Follow the directions provided for the questions.

1. Complete the following one-sentence summary of the article using the lettered phrases from the phrase bank below. Write the letters on the lines.

> **Phrase bank:**
> a. a description of the bombing
> b. a description of how he was rescued
> c. what happened to Ng'ang'a after the blast

The article about the Nairobi bombing begins with _____,

goes on to explain _____, and ends with _____.

2. Look for the important ideas and events in paragraphs 8 and 9. Summarize those paragraphs in one or two sentences.

_____

_____

_____

_____

3. Read the statement from the article below. Then read the paraphrase of that statement. Choose the reason that best tells why the paraphrase does not say the same thing as the statement.

Statement: "If they disrupted the balance of the rubble, the entire pile of steel and concrete could collapse."

Paraphrase: If they moved the rubble, it could fall and kill the people trapped underneath.

☐ a. Paraphrase says too much.

☐ b. Paraphrase doesn't say enough.

☐ c. Paraphrase doesn't agree with the statement from the article.

_____ Number of correct answers

Record your personal assessment of your work on the Critical Thinking Chart on page 150.

Critical Thinking

Put an X in the box next the the correct answer for questions 1 and 3. Follow the directions provided for questions 2, 4, and 5.

1. Which of the following statements from the article is an opinion rather than a fact?

☐ a. People on the other side of town felt their buildings shudder.

☐ b. "I was expecting to wait two or three days," he said.

☐ c. He had lost all sense of time.

2. Choose from the letters below to correctly complete the following statement. Write the letters on the lines.

According to the article, a bomb caused _____ to _____, and the effect was _____.

a. that many people were buried under the rubble

b. the Ufundi Cooperative House

c. collapse

3. From what Ng'ang'a said about Rose, you can conclude that

☐ a. her injuries were worse than Ng'ang'a's.

☐ b. she was selfish.

☐ c. rescuers never found her.

4. Using the information in the article, list at least 2 ways in which Ng'ang'a and Rose's situations were similar and two ways in which they were different.

Similarities

_____

_____

_____

Differences

_____

_____

_____

5. Which paragraphs provide evidence from the article to support your answer to question 4?

_____

_____ Number of correct answers

Record your personal assessment of your work on the Critical Thinking Chart on page 150.

Personal Response

A question I would like answered by Gaitara Ng'ang'a is

_____

_____

_____

Self-Assessment

Before reading this article, I already knew

_____

_____

_____

Firebomb on the Subway

The New York subway carries millions of people to their destinations every day. Unfortunately, the crowded subway cars have been the targets of violent attacks, such as Edward Leary's firebomb explosion.

Denfield Otto was running late. The off-duty transit officer rushed onto the New York City subway on December 21, 1994. As he hopped on the sixth car of the Number 4 train headed to Brooklyn, he hoped he wouldn't be late for choir practice at St. Philip's Church. But Otto didn't make it to the church that day. A firebomb interrupted his plans.

2   The Number 4 train was crowded with office workers and holiday shoppers laden with gifts. Most of these people were on their way somewhere. But one person on board

had a different agenda. He was Edward Leary, a 49-year-old man from New Jersey. Leary wanted to kill or maim as many passengers as possible. It was all part of a twisted scheme he had to extort money from the transit system. Once he had killed some people, he planned to use the threat of more violence to collect big sums of money. A week earlier Leary had made a test run. He set off a firebomb in a different train. That fire badly burned two students.

3   Now Leary was on the Number 4. There was nothing unusual in the way he was dressed. He wore a hat, a dark blue coat, blue jeans, and sneakers. In his hands he carried a paper bag. Witnesses later told the police that they saw him fumbling with something inside the bag. Some people also noticed an odd smell, like gasoline. One woman moved away from Leary after seeing his bag and smelling the gasoline. But Denfield Otto, who was just 15 feet away, never noticed Leary.

4   Shortly after 1:30 P.M., the Number 4 pulled into Fulton Street Station. Everything seemed normal. But just as the train doors began to open, commuters heard a loud pop. To some it sounded like a cherry bomb. Then suddenly a ball of fire engulfed the train and its passengers. People's clothing and hair caught fire. Some started running around, wildly beating their clothes to kill the flames. Others rolled on the floor of the train or on the concrete platform in an attempt to snuff out the fire.

5   "Everyone was on fire and they were screaming and hollering and running," recalled Alma Foster. "It was the scariest thing. I didn't think I was going to make it. I thought I was going to get trampled."

6   When Denfield Otto saw the blaze, he dashed out the door and ran for a token booth. There he grabbed a fire extinguisher and ran back to train. He aimed it at two people who were lying on the floor of the train in flames. He extinguished the fire on both of them, in all likelihood saving their lives.

7   Meanwhile James Nobles, a token clerk, instantly saw what was happening. He hit the emergency switch, bringing police and medics quickly to the rescue. Everyone started working together. As Denfield Otto said, "Black and white, it made no difference. One guy burning was a black guy, and white and black were beating out the flames."

8   New Yorkers hailed Otto as a hero. Mayor Rudolph Giuliani praised his "immediate and brave response." President Bill Clinton called to congratulate him. A reporter asked Otto how it felt to be a hero. He shrugged his shoulders and said that he didn't see himself as a hero. "I only did my job," he answered.

9   Despite his modesty, Otto *was* a hero. So were several others. Total strangers risked their lives to beat out the fires on people next to them. Mary McMurry was one such hero. She came to the aid of three fellow passengers. "They were burning, laying there burning," she said. "Whatever we could do, we rolled them on the ground and threw jackets on them [to squelch the flames]."

10   Curt Jackson was one of the burn victims. Still, that didn't stop him from helping others. "All I remember was a bang going off," he said later from his hospital bed. "[Then] I felt my face burning." He ran from the

train in pain. But when Jackson saw another person burning on the platform, he stopped and put out the fire with his jacket.

11 Miraculously no one was killed. Still, 50 people were burned, four critically. Alina Badia, a medic, was one of many who rushed to the station. The scene there looked like a war zone. "We pulled up and it was like a swarm of people with burns," said Badia. "Their skin was blackened . . . the burns were so deep they were bleeding from them. Their clothes were stuck to their bodies . . . one man, when we cut his gloves off, his skin came with it."

12 One of the victims, it turned out, was Edward Leary himself. It seemed that his homemade bomb had gone off before he intended. Badly burned, Leary escaped by hopping onto another subway train. He then switched to a second train. Finally the police spotted him a mile away in Brooklyn. At first they thought he

was another victim. His sneakers and jeans were burned. So was two-thirds of his body. Some of the skin on his face was peeling off. The police quickly called an ambulance to rush him to the hospital.

13 En route to the hospital, ambulance workers heard a radio description of the suspect. He was white, about 200 pounds, between 40 and 50 years old, wearing blue jeans and a dark blue coat. A police officer who was riding in the ambulance looked back at Leary. "Wait a minute," he said to another officer. "That sounds like the guy that we have."

14 Leary was quickly arrested. The police charged him with 45 counts of attempted murder. On May 2, 1995, a court found him guilty of the charges. Judge Rena Uviller sentenced him to 94 years in prison. That was the maximum sentence allowed by law. In her final statement, Judge Uviller said, "Evil exists in this world. There is no

reason for it. It's just there. And we are looking at it in the person of Edward Leary."

15 There is also good in the world. We see that when we look at people such as Mary McMurry, Curt Jackson, Alina Badia, and Denfield Otto.

If you have been timed while reading this article, enter your reading time below. Then turn to the Words-per-Minute Table on page 147 and look up your reading speed (words per minute). Enter your reading speed on the graph on page 148.

Reading Time: Lesson 14

_____ : _____
Minutes   Seconds

A Finding the Main Idea

One statement below expresses the main idea of the article. One statement is too general, or too broad. The other statement explains only part of the article; it is too narrow. Label the statements using the following key:

M—Main Idea   **B—Too Broad**   **N—Too Narrow**

_____ 1. Hoping to get money from the transit system, Edward Leary set off a firebomb on a New York subway car, injuring about 50 people.

_____ 2. Edward Leary's firebomb went off too early, and he was injured in the explosion.

_____ 3. A firebomb on a New York subway car injured many people.

_____ Score 15 points for a correct M answer.

_____ Score 5 points for each correct B or N answer.

_____ **Total Score:** Finding the Main Idea

B Recalling Facts

How well do you remember the facts in the article? Put an X in the box next to the answer that correctly completes each statement about the article.

1. Edward Leary planned to set off a firebomb in the New York subway because he
   ☐ a. didn't like the transit system.
   ☐ b. wanted to commit suicide.
   ☐ c. wanted to get money from the transit system.

2. On the Number 4 subway train, some people noticed Leary because he
   ☐ a. was holding a bag that smelled like gasoline.
   ☐ b. was dressed strangely.
   ☐ c. looked nervous.

3. When Leary's bomb exploded,
   ☐ a. he was not on the train.
   ☐ b. people's clothes and hair caught on fire.
   ☐ c. the train was on its way to Fulton Street Station.

4. When transit officer Denfield Otto saw the fire, he
   ☐ a. hit the emergency switch.
   ☐ b. grabbed a fire extinguisher and put out the fire on two people.
   ☐ c. threw his jacket on top of one of the victims.

5. The police found Edward Leary
   ☐ a. getting onto another subway train.
   ☐ b. as he was on his way to the hospital.
   ☐ c. about a mile away from the site of the bombing.

Score 5 points for each correct answer.

_____ **Total Score:** Recalling Facts

C | Making Inferences

When you combine your own experience with information from a text to draw a conclusion that is not directly stated in that text, you are making an inference. Below are five statements that may or may not be inferences based on information in the article. Label the statements using the following key:

C—Correct Inference   F—Faulty Inference

_____ 1. Edward Leary used to work for the New York transit system.

_____ 2. Gasoline can be used to make bombs.

_____ 3. If your clothes catch on fire, rolling on the ground can put it out.

_____ 4. Four people eventually died from their burns.

_____ 5. Edward Leary did not have much money.

Score 5 points for each correct answer.

_____ **Total Score:** Making Inferences

D | Using Words Precisely

Each numbered sentence below contains an underlined word or phrase from the article. Following the sentence are three definitions. One definition is closest to the meaning of the underlined word. One definition is opposite or nearly opposite. Label those two definitions using the following key; do not label the remaining definition.

C—Closest   O—Opposite or Nearly Opposite

1. The Number 4 train was crowded with office workers and holiday shoppers laden with gifts.

_____ a. loaded with

_____ b. carrying

_____ c. free of

2. Leary wanted to kill or maim as many passengers as possible.

_____ a. frighten

_____ b. help

_____ c. injure

3. Then suddenly a ball of fire engulfed the train and its passengers.

_____ a. avoided

_____ b. surrounded

_____ c. burned

4. "We rolled them on the ground and threw jackets on them [to squelch the flames]."

_____ a. put out

_____ b. cover

_____ c. start

5. The police charged him with 45 counts of <u>attempted</u> murder.

_____ a. planned

_____ b. tried

_____ c. successful

_____ Score 3 points for each correct C answer.

_____ Score 2 points for each correct O answer.

_____ **Total Score:** Using Words Precisely

Enter the four total scores in the spaces below, and add them together to find your Reading Comprehension Score. Then record your score on the graph on page 149.

Score	Question Type	Lesson 14
_____	Finding the Main Idea	
_____	Recalling Facts	
_____	Making Inferences	
_____	Using Words Precisely	
_____	**Reading Comprehension Score**	

Author's Approach

Put an X in the box next to the correct answer.

1. The main purpose of the first paragraph is to

☐ a. get the reader's attention.

☐ b. give background information about Denfield Otto.

☐ c. inform the reader about the New York subway.

2. The authors probably wrote this article in order to

☐ a. inform the reader about the firebomb on the New York subway.

☐ b. express an opinion about Edward Leary.

☐ c. persuade the reader not to ride the subway in New York.

3. Which of the following statements from the article best describes Denfield Otto?

☐ a. Denfield Otto was running late.

☐ b. When Denfield Otto saw the blaze, he dashed out the door and ran for a token booth.

☐ c. He shrugged his shoulders and said that he didn't see himself as a hero.

_____ Number of correct answers

Record your personal assessment of your work on the Critical Thinking Chart on page 150.

Summarizing and Paraphrasing

Follow the directions provided for question 1. Put an X in the box next to the correct answer for questions 2 and 3.

1. Reread paragraph 2 in the article. Below, write a summary of the paragraph in no more than 25 words.

_____

_____

_____

_____

Reread your summary and decide whether it covers the important ideas in the paragraph. Next, decide how to shorten the summary to 15 words or less without leaving out any essential information. Write this summary below.

_____

_____

_____

2. Read the statement from the article below. Then read the paraphrase of that statement. Choose the reason that best tells why the paraphrase does not say the same thing as the statement.

   Statement: "Witnesses later told police that they saw him fumbling with something inside the bag."

   Paraphrase: Witnesses told the police that Leary almost dropped the bag when he tried to reach inside it.

   ☐ a. Paraphrase says too much.

   ☐ b. Paraphrase doesn't say enough.

   ☐ c. Paraphrase doesn't agree with the statement from the article.

3. Choose the best one-sentence paraphrase for the following sentence from the article: "It was all part of a twisted scheme he had to extort money from the transit system."

   ☐ a. It was all part of a crooked plan he had to raise money for the transit system.

   ☐ b. It was all part of a sick plan he had to get money from the transit system.

   ☐ c. It was all part of his plot to make money.

_____ Number of correct answers

Record your personal assessment of your work on the Critical Thinking Chart on page 150.

Critical Thinking

Follow the directions provided for questions 1, 3, and 4. Put an X in the box next to the correct answer for questions 2 and 5.

1. For each statement below, write *O* if it expresses an opinion or *F* if it expresses a fact.

    _____ a. One woman moved away from Leary after seeing his bag and smelling the gasoline.

    _____ b. "I thought I was going to get trampled."

    _____ c. He shrugged his shoulders and said that he didn't see himself as a hero.

2. From the information in the article, you can predict that

    ☐ a. Edward Leary never carried out his plan.

    ☐ b. Denfield Otto never rode the subway again.

    ☐ c. there have been more firebombs set off on the New York subway since Leary was arrested.

3. Which paragraphs provide evidence from the article to support your answer to question 2?

    _____

4. Choose from the letters below to correctly complete the following statement. Write the letters on the lines.

    According to paragraph 12, _____ because _____.

    a. it went off too soon

    b. he was found a mile away in Brooklyn

    c. Edward Leary was burned by his own bomb

5. What did you have to do to answer question 4?

    ☐ a. find a cause (why something happened)

    ☐ b. find an opinion (what someone thinks about something)

    ☐ c. find a purpose (why something is done)

> _____ Number of correct answers
>
> Record your personal assessment of your work on the Critical Thinking Chart on page 150.

Personal Response

How do you think Edward Leary felt when Judge Uviller gave her final statement?

_____

_____

Self-Assessment

The part I found most difficult about the article was

_____

_____

I found this difficult because

_____

_____

Escape Artist

Damon J. Gause didn't want to die. He didn't want to be a prisoner, either. Gause was a U.S. lieutenant during World War II. He was stationed in Bataan, a province on the Philippine island of Luzon. In April 1942 Japanese soldiers overran Bataan. They killed or captured most of the Americans there. Lieutenant Gause was taken prisoner.

2   Japanese guards forced Gause and about 300 others into a prison camp. They gave them no food or water. After two days, Gause had suffered enough. He decided to make a run for it. First, he managed to kill his prison guard. Then he ran out through a strip of jungle. He was headed for Manila Bay and the ocean beyond. Japanese soldiers chased after him. They sent bullets whistling past his head. Luckily, Gause later wrote, "they were bad shots." He reached

Lieutenant Damon "Rocky" Gause and Captain William Lloyd Osborne stand in front of the 20-foot boat in which they traveled 3,200 miles from the Philippine Islands to Australia during World War II.

Manila Bay and swam out to sea, bullets still splashing on all sides.

3   It took Gause hours to swim the three miles to the Philippine island of Corregidor. At the time, this small island was under American rule. Gause spent some time in a Corregidor hospital, recovering from exhaustion. Soon, though, he was back in action. He left his bed to take command of a machine gun squad.

4   Meanwhile, Corregidor was becoming less and less safe. Each day the Japanese lobbed shells in from across the bay. The Japanese had many more men than the Americans had. It was only a matter of time before they invaded the small island. On the night of May 4, they did exactly that. The Americans had no choice but to surrender.

5   Gause realized he was in big trouble. The Japanese knew he had escaped from them once before. They would be especially hard on him now, so he felt he had no choice. He had to get away from Corregidor before the Japanese saw him.

6   As his fellow soldiers were surrendering, Gause made his move.

Lieutenant Arranzaso, a Filipino pilot, went with him. The two men found an old boat. Under the cover of darkness, they paddled out to sea. They headed for Luzon, hoping to avoid Bataan and other Japanese-held parts of the island.

7   As they bobbed along in the waves, Gause and Arranzaso heard a voice yelling at them in English. It came from the shore of Corregidor. Arranzaso worried that it might be a trick. He feared that the voice belonged to a Japanese soldier. But after shouting out some questions and hearing the answers, Gause decided to trust his instincts. He allowed the man to swim out to the boat. As it turned out, he was a Filipino scout who was also trying to escape. The scout joined them on the boat, and they continued on their way.

8   The sea was rough, and the men made little progress. By dawn they were only about one-third of the way to Luzon. Daylight also meant danger. Soon a Japanese plane spotted them and opened fire. Gause and the other two men jumped over the side. Their boat was struck by a hail of

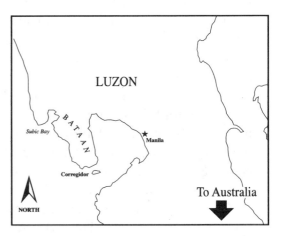

bullets. Then Arranzaso cried out, "I've been hit."

9   With his sock, Gause tried to stop Arranzaso's wound from bleeding. The scout retrieved a couple of bamboo poles from the ruined boat. Using the poles for support, the three men began swimming.

10   They got within a few hundred yards of Luzon, but by then all three were worn out. They hadn't eaten in two days and hadn't had any fresh water in more than 24 hours. In addition, the current was very strong. It was becoming almost impossible to stay afloat. The scout, using his last bit of strength, made it to the shore. He went looking for a boat to rescue Gause and Arranzaso.

11   Gause stayed in the water with the badly wounded Arranzaso. Arranzaso had his arms draped over the bamboo poles. He had swallowed a lot of sea water. He knew that he could never swim all the way to shore. But he also knew that Gause would not leave him. He was afraid Gause would die, too, unless he got to shore soon. So Arranzaso gave his money belt to Gause. He told Gause to give the money to his mother. Arranzaso then blessed himself and said, "Sir, my game is up." With that, he released the poles and sank beneath the surface.

12   Gause dove after him, trying to save him, but it was no use. The swirling currents were too strong. "I knew that Arranzaso had sacrificed his life to save mine," said Gause.

13   Now Gause had no reason to wait. With a final burst of energy, he began to swim for the shore. But a powerful current pushed him mostly sideways. "My arms were threshing the water aimlessly," Gause wrote. "I was about to give up when a knee dug into the sand." Gause thought his mind might be playing a trick on him. So he took a few more strokes. "Then I carefully let my legs drop and stretched my arms downward and I felt land. I plodded twenty feet up the beach and crumpled . . . . I fell into an exhausted sleep."

14   Luckily, the Japanese didn't find him. But his troubles were far from over. He was still in enemy territory. After resting and getting some strength back, Gause met Captain William Lloyd Osborne. Osborne was another American on the run. Together, the two men decided to flee south to Australia. Most people would never have tried this. After all, Australia was 3,000 miles away. But Gause believed they could make it.

15   With help from friendly Filipinos, he and Osborne found an old sailboat. It had a motor that worked only some of the time. They had no charts, no instruments, and little fuel. They solved the fuel problem by stealing some from a Japanese fuel depot. They made a Japanese flag with cloth they had found. The flag would save their lives more than once.

16   Gause and Osborne knew three words of Japanese: "Long live Japan!" Whenever a warship came near, they posed as local fishermen. First, they would run the Japanese flag up the pole. Then they would wave their arms and shout, "Long live Japan!" They managed to safely pass several Japanese ships in this way.

17   Slowly, the men made their way from island to island. They passed countless sharks in the water. From time to time, they managed to hook and kill one. That gave them raw shark meat to eat. Most of the islands had no fresh water, so the men had little to drink but coconut milk.

18   Still, their luck was very good. Once they landed on a tiny island named Culion. It was used as a leper colony. One of the staff there was an American engineer. He fixed the motor on their boat.

19   At last, after 159 days at sea and 3,000 miles, Gause and Osborne made it to Australia. They were flown to see General Douglas MacArthur. A barefoot Lieutenant Damon Gause saluted MacArthur and said that he "reported from Corregidor." The stunned general could only mutter, "Well, I'll be damned."

If you have been timed while reading this article, enter your reading time below. Then turn to the Words-per-Minute Table on page 147 and look up your reading speed (words per minute). Enter your reading speed on the graph on page 148.

Reading Time: Lesson 15

_____ : _____
Minutes   Seconds

A | Finding the Main Idea

One statement below expresses the main idea of the article. One statement is too general, or too broad. The other statement explains only part of the article; it is too narrow. Label the statements using the following key:

M—Main Idea   **B—Too Broad**   **N—Too Narrow**

_____ 1. Lt. Damon Gause escaped from the Japanese several times during his army service.

_____ 2. Lt. Damon Gause made several daring escapes in the Philippines during World War II.

_____ 3. Lt. Damon Gause escaped from the Philippines during World War II and made it all the way to Australia after a 3,000-mile trip in a small boat.

_____ Score 15 points for a correct M answer.

_____ Score 5 points for each correct B or N answer.

_____ **Total Score:** Finding the Main Idea

B | Recalling Facts

How well do you remember the facts in the article? Put an X in the box next to the answer that correctly completes each statement about the article.

1. Gause escaped from a Japanese prison camp
   - ☐ a. on the island of Corregidor.
   - ☐ b. by killing a prison guard.
   - ☐ c. twice.

2. Gause and Arranzaso left Corregidor
   - ☐ a. at night.
   - ☐ b. to head for Bataan.
   - ☐ c. before the Americans surrendered.

3. Arranzaso let himself sink into the ocean because he
   - ☐ a. couldn't hold himself up any longer.
   - ☐ b. knew that otherwise Gause would not leave him.
   - ☐ c. thought Gause would save him.

4. When Lieutenant Gause and Captain Osborne decided to leave the Philippines, they
   - ☐ a. stole a boat from the Japanese.
   - ☐ b. took a lot of food with them.
   - ☐ c. headed to Australia in an old sailboat.

5. While they were at sea, Gause and Osborne managed to escape the Japanese
   - ☐ a. with the help of local fishermen.
   - ☐ b. by pretending to be Japanese fishermen.
   - ☐ c. by going from island to island.

_____ Score 5 points for each correct answer.

_____ **Total Score:** Recalling Facts

C | Making Inferences

When you combine your own experience with information from a text to draw a conclusion that is not directly stated in that text, you are making an inference. Below are five statements that may or may not be inferences based on information in the article. Label the statements using the following key:

C—Correct Inference   F—Faulty Inference

_____ 1. Many of the soldiers in the Japanese prison camps died.

_____ 2. Gause was a good swimmer.

_____ 3. Captain Osborne had also escaped from Corregidor.

_____ 4. People with leprosy are still kept on secluded islands.

_____ 5. Gause and Osborne did not take any food with them on their trip to Australia.

Score 5 points for each correct answer.

_____ **Total Score:** Making Inferences

D | Using Words Precisely

Each numbered sentence below contains an underlined word or phrase from the article. Following the sentence are three definitions. One definition is closest to the meaning of the underlined word. One definition is opposite or nearly opposite. Label those two definitions using the following key; do not label the remaining definition.

C—Closest   O—Opposite or Nearly Opposite

1. Each day the Japanese <u>lobbed</u> shells in from across the bay.

_____ a. caught

_____ b. shot

_____ c. threw

2. The Americans had no choice but to <u>surrender</u>.

_____ a. give up

_____ b. resist

_____ c. fight

3. The <u>swirling</u> currents were too strong.

_____ a. racing

_____ b. straight

_____ c. twisting

4. "I plodded twenty feet up the beach and <u>crumpled</u> . . . "

_____ a. stood up

_____ b. cried

_____ c. collapsed

5. Together, the two men decided to <u>flee</u> south to Australia.

_____ a. travel

_____ b. escape

_____ c. return

_____ Score 3 points for each correct C answer.

_____ Score 2 points for each correct O answer.

_____ **Total Score:** Using Words Precisely

Enter the four total scores in the spaces below, and add them together to find your Reading Comprehension Score. Then record your score on the graph on page 149.

Score	Question Type	Lesson 15
_____	Finding the Main Idea	
_____	Recalling Facts	
_____	Making Inferences	
_____	Using Words Precisely	
_____	**Reading Comprehension Score**	

Author's Approach

Put an X in the box next to the correct answer.

1. The authors use the first sentence of the article to

☐ a. inform the reader about Damon Gause.

☐ b. get the reader's attention.

☐ c. entertain the reader.

2. What is the authors' purpose in writing "Escape Artist"?

☐ a. to describe Damon Gause's amazing escapes

☐ b. to inform the reader about the events in the Philippines during World War II

☐ c. to express an opinion about Damon Gause

3. What do the authors imply by saying, "The stunned general could only mutter, 'Well, I'll be damned.'"?

☐ a. General MacArthur didn't like Gause and Osborne.

☐ b. General MacArthur was very surprised that Gause and Osborne had made it to Australia from Corregidor.

☐ c. General MacArthur wasn't very interested in Gause and Osborne.

_____ Number of correct answers

Record your personal assessment of your work on the Critical Thinking Chart on page 150.

Summarizing and Paraphrasing

Follow the directions provided for questions 1 and 2. Put an X in the box next to the correct answer for question 3.

1. Look for the important ideas and events in paragraphs 6 and 7. Summarize those paragraphs in one or two sentences.

_____

_____

_____

2. Reread paragraph 17 in the article. Below, write a summary of the paragraph in no more than 25 words.

_____

_____

_____

_____

Reread your summary and decide whether it covers the important ideas in the paragraph. Next, decide how to shorten the summary to 15 words or less without leaving out any essential information. Write this summary below.

_____

_____

3. Choose the sentence that correctly restates the following sentence from the article: "In April 1942 Japanese soldiers overran Bataan."

☐ a. In April 1942 Japanese soldiers flew over Bataan.

☐ b. In April 1942 Japanese soldiers took over Bataan.

☐ c. In April 1942 Japanese soldiers landed on Bataan.

_____ Number of correct answers

Record your personal assessment of your work on the Critical Thinking Chart on page 150.

Critical Thinking

Put an X in the box next to the correct answer for questions 1, 3, and 5. Follow the directions provided for questions 2 and 4.

1. Which of the following statements from the article is an opinion rather than a fact?

☐ a. It took Gause hours to swim the three miles to the Philippine island of Corregidor.

☐ b. He feared the voice belonged to a Japanese soldier.

☐ c. With his sock, Gause tried to stop Arranzaso's wound from bleeding.

2. Choose from the letters below to correctly complete the following statement. Write the letters on the lines.

   According to paragraph 2, _____ because _____.

   a. Gause was able to escape from the Japanese

   b. he ran through the jungle

   c. they were bad shots

3. What was the cause of Gause's leaving for Luzon by boat?

   ☐ a. Lieutenant Arranzaso wanted to escape.

   ☐ b. He wanted to leave the army.

   ☐ c. He thought the Japanese would be especially hard on him if they caught him again.

4. Which paragraphs provide evidence from the article to support your answer to question 3?

   _____

5. Into which of the following theme categories would this story fit?

   ☐ a. soldiers in World War II

   ☐ b. Japanese prison camps

   ☐ c. great escapes

   _____ Number of correct answers

   Record your personal assessment of your work on the Critical Thinking Chart on page 150.

Personal Response

What was most surprising or interesting to you about this article?

_____

_____

_____

_____

Self-Assessment

From reading this article, I have learned

_____

_____

_____

Compare and Contrast

Think about the articles you have read in Unit Three. Pick three articles that show someone helping a person who is in danger. Write the titles of the articles in the first column of the chart below. Use information you have learned from the articles to fill in the empty boxes in the chart.

Title	Who needed to be helped in this article? Why did they need help?	Who helped someone in this article? What did they do?	Pick one of the people from this article. What would you have done if you had been in the same situation as this person?

Which of these situations would you least like to have been in? Why?

_____

_____

Words-per-Minute Table

Unit Three

Directions: If you were timed while reading an article, refer to the Reading Time you recorded in the box at the end of the article. Use this Words-per-Minute Table to determine your reading speed for that article. Then plot your reading speed on the graph on page 148.

Lesson No. of Words	11 1051	12 1203	13 1104	14 1038	15 1190	Seconds
1:30	701	802	736	692	793	90
1:40	631	722	662	623	714	100
1:50	573	656	602	566	649	110
2:00	526	602	552	519	595	120
2:10	485	555	510	479	549	130
2:20	450	516	473	445	510	140
2:30	420	481	442	415	476	150
2:40	394	451	414	389	446	160
2:50	371	425	390	366	420	170
3:00	350	401	368	346	397	180
3:10	332	380	349	328	376	190
3:20	315	361	331	311	357	200
3:30	300	344	315	297	340	210
3:40	287	328	301	283	325	220
3:50	274	314	288	271	310	230
4:00	263	301	276	260	298	240
4:10	252	289	265	249	286	250
4:20	243	278	255	240	275	260
4:30	234	267	245	231	264	270
4:40	225	258	237	222	255	280
4:50	217	249	228	215	246	290
5:00	210	241	221	208	238	300
5:10	203	233	214	201	230	310
5:20	197	226	207	195	223	320
5:30	191	219	201	189	216	330
5:40	185	212	195	183	210	340
5:50	180	206	189	178	204	350
6:00	175	201	184	173	198	360
6:10	170	195	179	168	193	370
6:20	166	190	174	164	188	380
6:30	162	185	170	160	183	390
6:40	158	180	166	156	179	400
6:50	154	176	162	152	174	410
7:00	150	172	158	148	170	420
7:10	147	168	154	145	166	430
7:20	143	164	151	142	162	440
7:30	140	160	147	138	159	450
7:40	137	157	144	135	155	460
7:50	134	154	141	133	152	470
8:00	131	150	138	130	149	480

Minutes and Seconds

Plotting Your Progress: Reading Speed

Unit Three

Directions: If you were timed while reading an article, write your words-per-minute rate for that article in the box under the number of the lesson. Then plot your reading speed on the graph by putting a small X on the line directly above the number of the lesson, across from the number of words per minute you read. As you mark your speed for each lesson, graph your progress by drawing a line to connect the X's.

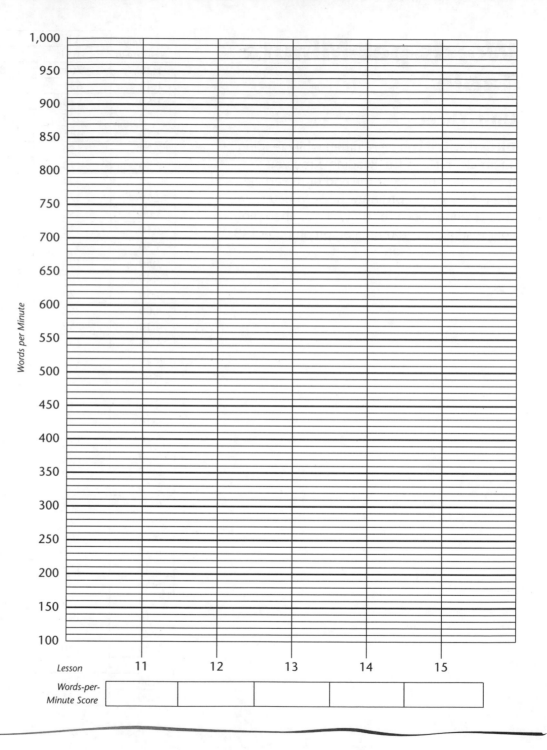

Lesson	11	12	13	14	15
Words-per-Minute Score					

Plotting Your Progress: Reading Comprehension

Unit Three

Directions: Write your Reading Comprehension score for each lesson in the box under the number of the lesson. Then plot your score on the graph by putting a small X on the line directly above the number of the lesson and across from the score you earned. As you mark your score for each lesson, graph your progress by drawing a line to connect the X's.

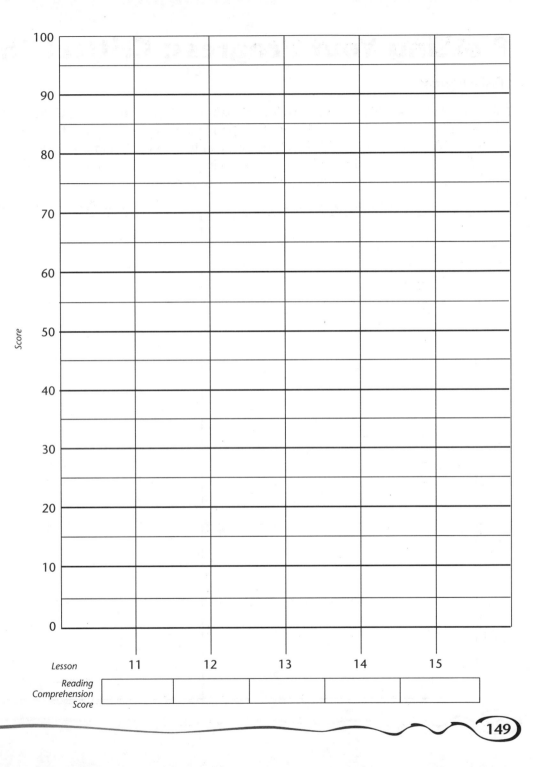

Plotting Your Progress: Critical Thinking

Unit Three

Directions: Work with your teacher to evaluate your responses to the Critical Thinking questions for each lesson. Then fill in the appropriate spaces in the chart below. For each lesson and each type of Critical Thinking question, do the following: Mark a minus sign (–) in the box to indicate areas in which you feel you could improve. Mark a plus sign (+) to indicate areas in which you feel you did well. Mark a minus-slash-plus sign (–/+) to indicate areas in which you had mixed success. Then write any comments you have about your performance, including ideas for improvement.

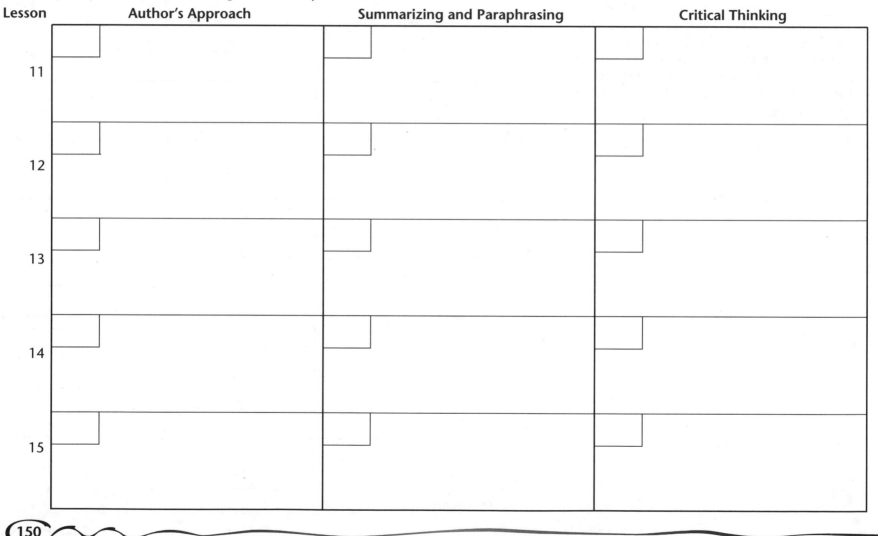

Lesson	Author's Approach	Summarizing and Paraphrasing	Critical Thinking
11			
12			
13			
14			
15			

Photo Credits